CHRISTEN KØBKE
Danish Master of Light

DAVID JACKSON
with a contribution by Kasper Monrad

CHRISTEN KØBKE

Danish Master of Light

National Galleries of Scotland, Edinburgh
in association with The National Gallery, London

Published by the Trustees of the National Galleries
of Scotland, Edinburgh, to accompany the exhibition
Christen Købke: Danish Master of Light held at the
National Gallery, London from 17 March to 13 June 2010
and at the National Gallery Complex, Edinburgh, from
4 July to 3 October 2010. The exhibition is organised by
the National Gallery, London and the National Gallery of
Scotland, Edinburgh.

ISBN 978 1 906270 27 8
© The Trustees of the National Galleries of Scotland 2010

Designed and typeset in Aldus and Juliana by Dalrymple
Printed on 150gsm Perigord Matt and bound by
by Butler Tanner and Dennis, Frome, Somerset

The proceeds from the sale of this book go towards
supporting the National Galleries of Scotland, a charity
registered in Scotland (no.SC003728).
www.nationalgalleries.org

*Unless otherwise stated all works illustrated are
by Christen Købke.*

Front cover: Detail from *View Outside the North Gate of the
Citadel*, 1834 [27], Ny Carlsberg Glyptotek, Copenhagen

Frontispiece: Detail from *View from the Loft
of the Grain Store at the Bakery in the Citadel*, 1831 [22]
Statens Museum for Kunst, Copenhagen

Back cover: *View from Dosseringen near the Sortedam
Lake Looking towards Nørrebro*, c.1838 [58],
Statens Museum for Kunst, Copenhagen

Research supported by

 Arts & Humanities
Research Council

Preface by Queen Margrethe II of Denmark

The artist Christen Købke epitomises some of the finest qualities of the Danish Golden Age. The nature of that era becomes apparent when we remember that Hans Christian Andersen and Søren Kierkegaard were his contemporaries. We are ready to accept them as small-town geniuses in tiny Copenhagen of those days just as we are aware that this cultural heyday in Denmark would not have been possible without influence from outside. Yet as we trace the development of this Golden Age through its formative years up towards 1848, we do feel that the era expresses something which we may name truly Danish.

Christen Købke found his true self as well as his artistic themes in his close surroundings. He did so with a personality and an inner strength of character which did not make him a particular focus of attention among his contemporary artistic friends, but which have nevertheless caused his standing to grow ever since. He was not John Constable, nor Caspar David Friedrich, but in a strange way he was in some respects like them, just as one might find, without any real explanation, a flower growing where no-one would have expected it.

In Denmark we have taken quiet pleasure in this, but since there is nothing better than to be able to share, it gives us even more enjoyment that in recent years Købke has come to occupy a place of honour in the context of the period between Napoleon and the European ideals of freedom – the period to which Købke, on his own Danish premises, belonged.

Købke's works are small marvels in paint, which bring us close to the real life of that time; from his depictions of the close circle of the family, to all of God's creation seen in everyday fragments of nature, and also in scenes from Copenhagen, which had been lying tucked in behind its green ramparts for several hundred years. It is a source of great pride to us in Denmark that Købke's work is attracting more and more attention internationally, and especially that his art has been met with such sympathy. Thus it is a great pleasure for me to be the patron of this exhibition, which is certain to deepen the appreciation of Købke's paintings in both London and Edinburgh, and will surely attract more visitors to Denmark's own great collections.

Directors' Foreword ⁓

British appreciation of Christen Købke, arguably Denmark's greatest painter, is relatively recent. In 1984, the National Gallery in London mounted a major exhibition of eighty-three Golden Age masterpieces from the Statens Museum for Kunst in Copenhagen. *Danish Painting: The Golden Age* was one of the first exhibitions outside Denmark to survey the art of this period of extraordinary cultural efflorescence. It included key works by the major figures, such as Jens Juel, Christoffer Wilhelm Eckersberg, Constantin Hansen and Wilhelm Bendz. Particularly admired by the visitors to this show were no fewer than nineteen paintings by Christen Købke. The London show anticipated exhibitions on similar themes which followed in Paris, New York, Washington DC, Los Angeles, Ottawa and Hamburg, so that now the Danish accomplishment must be taken into account in any assessment of international developments in nineteenth-century European painting.

The National Gallery followed up the exhibition with acquisitions of paintings by Købke in 1986 and 1993. The National Gallery of Scotland, Edinburgh, too, acquired works by this remarkable artist in 1989 and 2002. Now, twenty-six years after that pioneering exhibition, the two National Galleries join forces to examine in depth the work of the same Christen Købke whose deceptively simple, light-filled paintings elicited such appreciation in 1984 and continue to do so now that he is represented in our permanent collections. There is something so appealing about Købke's images of family and friends, and of daily routine in and around the Copenhagen he so rarely left in his short life, that visitors respond immediately and delightedly. It is as if we are being spoken to directly by a modest young painter who wants nothing more than to let us in on the unassuming charms of Danish life.

The story is more complicated than that. The early nineteenth century was a period of turmoil in Danish society. National self-awareness was playing an ever-larger role in the wake of territorial losses, financial hardship, and the depredations of war. British forces set fire to Copenhagen in 1807, and in 1813 the entire nation was forced into bankruptcy. If we know where to look, we see how Købke's art registers these discontents, how it shows us a curious, questioning culture in full social and economic transition. We are fortunate in having an expert guide to Købke's art and the Danish culture it reflects in Professor David Jackson of Leeds University, guest curator for the exhibition who has been assisted by Sine Krogh. The co-ordination of the exhibition has been ably managed by Christopher

Riopelle, curator of nineteenth-century art at the National Gallery, London. Such an ambitious undertaking could not have taken place without the extraordinary generosity and collaboration of colleagues in the major Danish art institutions. Kasper Monrad, Chief Curator, at the Statens Museum for Kunst must be singled out among them, not only as a contributor to the catalogue but as an invaluable advisor from the moment our project began. It is a pleasure to acknowledge and thank other colleagues who have agreed to lend work from their collections including: Bodil Busk Laursen, Director, Det Danske Kunstindustrimuseum (Danish Museum of Art & Design), Copenhagen; Marianne Saabye, Director, and Jan Gorm Madsen, Curator of Paintings and Drawings, The Hirschsprung Collection, Copenhagen; Henri Loyrette, Director, and Vincent Pomarède, Conservateur Général, Musée du Louvre, Paris; Nils Ohrt, Director, Nivaagaards Malerisamling/ Nivaagaard Picture Gallery; Flemming Friborg, Director and Anna Schram Vejlby, Curator, Ny Carlsberg Glyptotek, Copenhagen; Anne-Birgitte Fonsmark, Director, and Nanna Kronberg Frederiksen, Curator, Ordrupgaard Collection, Copenhagen; Finn Terman Frederiksen, Director, Randers Kunstmuseum, Randers; Kjeld von Folsach, Director, The David Collection; Anne Marie Nehammer, Mikkel Scharff, Head of Paintings Department, and Claus M. Smidt, Chairman of the Loans Committee, The Royal Danish Academy of Fine Arts, Copenhagen; Karsten Ohrt, Director, Statens Museum for Kunst, Copenhagen; and those lenders who wish to remain anonymous.

Exhibitions such as this require considerable commitment from many departments and we wish to extend thanks to all our colleagues who have worked so hard to make the exhibition a success, and we hope that this will be the first of many collaborative ventures. We also owe a debt of gratitude to our sponsors who have been generous with their support. We would like to thank The A.P. Møller and Chastine Mc-Kinney Møller Foundation, Copenhagen, for supporting the exhibition in London, and Alex and Rhona Callander for sponsoring the exhibition in Edinburgh.

Finally, we are most appreciative that through the efforts of His Excellency Birger Riis-Jørgensen, Ambassador of Denmark to the Court of St James's and Lone Brit Molloy of the Danish Embassy to the United Kingdom that the exhibition has received royal patronage from Her Majesty Queen Margrethe II of Denmark.

NICHOLAS PENNY *Director, The National Gallery, London*

JOHN LEIGHTON *Director-General, National Galleries of Scotland, Edinburgh*

MICHAEL CLARKE *Director, National Gallery of Scotland, Edinburgh*

AUTHOR'S ACKNOWLEDGEMENTS

In addition to those already acknowledged in the Directors' Foreword, I wish to thank several individuals and institutions personally. I have been the recipient of an enormous amount of help, kindness and generosity, collectively and individually and whilst I can thank them only briefly, their impact on this project has been extensive and significant: at Den Hirschsprungske Samling, Jan Gorm Madsen; at Kunstakademiet (The Royal Danish Academy of Fine Arts), Claus M. Smidt and Anne Marie Nehammer; at Kunstakademiets Bibliotek (The Royal Danish Academy Library), Dr Patrick Kragelund and Dr Elisabeth Kofod-Hansen; at Kunstindustrimuseet, Charlotte Malte; at Ny Carlsberg Glyptotek, Tine Blicher-Moritz and Line Clausen Pedersen; at the Ny Carlsberg Foundation, Hans Edvard Nørregård-Nielsen and at Statens Museum for Kunst, Peter Nørgaard Larsen. I wish also to thank the art historian, Mikael Wivel, and Michael Porsager, vicar at Ramløse Church, for their individual contributions to the work as it progressed. Through the Ny Carlsberg Foundation and its secretary Anne Krøigaard I was granted accomodation in Copenhagen at principal times during the realisation of the project, for which I am deeply thankful.

I am greatly indebted to the editorial input of Claire Young, Duncan Thomson and most particularly Janis Adams, in their conscientious shaping of this publication. My thanks also to those staff at the National Gallery in London and the National Gallery of Scotland in Edinburgh who have assisted me over the years, in particular the initial interest and unflagging enthusiasm of Chris Riopelle and Michael Clarke, as well as the generous assistance of Victoria Anthoni, Miranda Stacey, Karine Hocking and Nicola Freeman. I wish to extend my most heartfelt gratitude to Kasper Monrad at Statens Museum for Kunst, who has supported me throughout this project. His generous and enthusiastic assistance could not be bettered and it has been a privilege to have worked with such a noted scholar of Golden Age art history.

It has been my great good fortune to have secured as research assistant to this project the contribution of Sine Krogh. Her intellectual insight and dedication, astute professionalism and unwavering sense of humour have been of inestimable value. Whilst it has not been practicable to acknowledge her contributions at every turn, I have relied heavily upon her talents, without which this project would have been much diminished. This project was brought to fruition courtesy of a major research award from the Arts and Humanities Research Council, to whom I wish to express my sincere appreciation.

Finally, but most importantly, I wish to dedicate this work to my son, Daniel.

DAVID JACKSON

The Age of Købke ⤳

1 · *Self-portrait, c.*1833
Statens Museum for Kunst, Copenhagen

The moment comes when the man is there, the right man, the man of the moment.
SØREN KIERKEGAARD

The period roughly corresponding to the first half of the nineteenth century in Denmark, which has earned the sobriquet of the Danish 'Golden Age', is commonly portrayed as a serene idyll, an unruffled bourgeois Eden, during which time the nation reached a peak in terms of its cultural achievements and social development – to such an extent indeed that it eclipsed all that came subsequently and was enshrined as a reference point for excellence in Danish national life. In this respect it might be presumed that this was an inevitable process, the apex of a steady continuum, or the gradual progression of concerted endeavour towards a common objective. For some it must have seemed so, yet the Golden Age had put forth its roots during a period of unprecedented chaos and confusion, and at a time of intense introspection and public catharsis.

The swiftness with which Denmark's fortunes were reversed at this time must have been bewildering to those caught up in events, a crisis which would have been hard to foresee when viewed against the nation's long and prosperous history, on which rested a well-founded sense of public stability. The oldest kingdom in Europe, the Danes traced their history to settlements predating both Bronze and Iron ages, and thence through the period of Viking domination during the eighth to eleventh centuries, which established them as feared and victorious colonisers across large sectors of the globe. Through exchange and commerce Denmark evolved from pagan conquerors to be united and officially Christianised in the year 965, becoming a major naval and trading power with influence throughout the Baltic. At various times the nation included Iceland, Norway and southern Sweden, and whilst wars saw these periodically change hands, Denmark prospered and Copenhagen grew into an important and increasingly cultured city.

From 1536, under Christian III, Denmark underwent a Lutheran Reformation, ousting the Catholic Church and strengthening the power of the king and the nobility. In 1660, after disastrous wars with Sweden which diminished Denmark's power, the influence of the nobility was curtailed and it became an absolutist monarchy (until 1849). The king, Frederik III, was declared the highest authority on earth, above all human laws, inferior

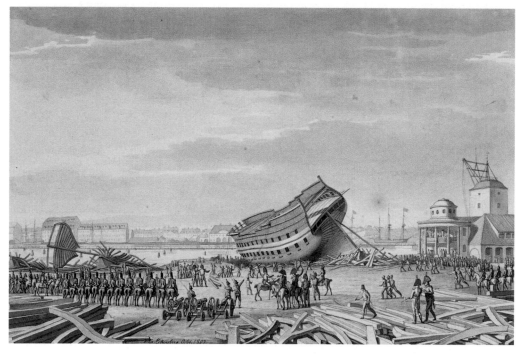

2 · C.A. Lorentzen, *The Most Terrifying Night: Copenhagen under Bombardment During the Night of 4–5 September 1807*, painted between 1807 and 1828
Statens Museum for Kunst, Copenhagen

3 · C.W. Eckersberg, *The Last Infamous Deed by the English in Copenhagen*, 1807
Department of Prints and Drawings, Statens Museum for Kunst, Copenhagen

to God alone. Supreme legislative, judicial and military authority resided solely in his hands, and in those of his successors. The monarchy ruled with the assistance of a growing civil service bureaucracy which ran various state departments while its imperial ambitions spread as far as colonies and trading posts in India, Ghana and the Danish West Indies.

Despite further clashes with the old enemy, Sweden, the eighteenth century brought prolonged peace and prosperity, the economics of which assisted in the liberation of the nation's peasants with the abolition of serfdom act of 1788.[1] Denmark also became the first European nation to abolish slave-trading, whilst simultaneously amassing a large merchant navy. The flourishing of trade, both abroad and through the tolls levied on vessels passing through the Øresund strait at Helsingør (effectively the gateway to the Baltic trading routes), had long boosted the nation's wealth to a near super power status. With hindsight, the political turbulence that preceded the nation's decline as the nineteenth century approached, seems ominously to have been presaged by two large fires in Copenhagen in 1794 and 1795. The first destroyed the royal residence of Christiansborg Palace; the second, or 'Great Fire', laid waste the city. But these were, if anything, merely a prelude.

The strategic importance of the Øresund meant that Denmark's political allegiance during the Napoleonic Wars required a near impossible feat of diplomacy, given that neither of the major warring factions, France and Britain, was prepared to accept Denmark's neutrality. Eventually Demark threw in its lot with France and disaster ensued, swiftly followed by economic meltdown. In 1801 its navy was crushed by Nelson during the Battle of Copenhagen, and in September 1807, without pretence at diplomacy, Copenhagen was subjected to a sustained assault by British forces that devastated it – the first ever bombardment targeted on civilians. The painter C.A. Lorentzen, who would become Købke's first tutor at the Royal Danish Academy of Fine Arts, was witness to the attack and left a dramatic record of the outrage [2]. Following the assault, the Danish fleet, amongst the largest in the world, was impounded and the Copenhagen shipyards were destroyed by British troops, an event recorded by C.W. Eckersberg [3], also to become a tutor of Købke's at the Academy and who was to assume a major and lasting significance in his artistic development. The city was subsequently blockaded, causing poverty and even famine. Frederik VI continued to pour the national budget into supporting Napoleon, with the result that inflation eventually exceeded 900% and in 1813 the nation declared bankruptcy. Unemployment soared, social distress intensified and wealthy commercial companies collapsed. When Napoleon fell, Sweden, allied with Britain, used the 1814 Treaty of Kiel to take Norway from Denmark, effectively terminating the little that remained of Danish power, a situation from which it never recovered. From here grew Denmark's self-assessment of its 'small and poor' nation status, as celebrated in popular song.[2]

Few Danes then would have considered they were living through a 'Golden Age', having experienced national disaster, defeat, humiliation and bankruptcy, which would end, eventually, in national disintegration. This was heralded in 1848–50 by the first of two wars with Germany over Schleswig and Holstein, and concluded in 1864 by the irretrievable loss of these territories, 'the definitive national trauma'.[3] Throughout this time an absolutist monarchy held sway under a militaristic rule and official censorship curtailed basic freedoms and visited harsh sentences on those who opposed the regime. The bright and airy images which have come to be regarded as quintessential of this period are sketched against a dark and sullied background, where the majority underclass lived in dire material want, enjoying an unhygienic cocktail of typhoid, malaria and high mortality rates in a culture resting upon a foundation of 'chronic bourgeois duality, double moral standards, hypocrisy and dissimulation behind a respectable Golden Age façade'.[4]

4 · *Portrait of the Artist's Mother, Cecilia Margrete, née Petersen*, 1829
National Gallery of Scotland, Edinburgh

And yet no small part of the Golden Age miracle rests on the astonishing rapidity with which the nation rallied and prospered following sufficient disasters to destroy it completely. Despite being still an overwhelmingly agricultural society (there was little industrialisation in Denmark until the mid-nineteenth century), the city of Copenhagen was the powerbase that generated and fostered this remarkable revival. Elegant neoclassical houses swiftly covered the sites of destruction, and from the early 1820s the nation's fortunes began to revive substantially. The reconstruction of Copenhagen got underway with major architectural projects, such as its new town hall, and the rebuilding of its cathedral and the Christiansborg Palace.

But the essence of the Golden Age was a restoration of the national psyche as the Danes took stock of themselves, and an almost inevitable resurgence of (a romantically-based) nationalism began to dominate the cultural agenda. Self-analysis turned to a searching for, and a pride in, those distinctive markers of nationhood that neither time nor political disasters could eradicate. As with many European powers, Denmark was substantially dominated by foreign cultural influences. Classical models prevailed in artistic and literary circles, whilst a strong Dutch influence was manifest in architecture, a legacy of reciprocal trade and competition with The Netherlands. A uniquely Danish or national culture seemed palpably missing, and even as late as the 1870s the writer Edmund Gosse noted during his travels in Denmark the historical absence of a distinctively Danish art prior to the nineteenth century.[5] A key aspect of the Golden Age was the will to promote a national culture, as well as the identification and reassessment of its antecedents. What perhaps most characterises the age was the unparalleled creative and innovative energy that was expended in such a brief time. Under an absolutist monarch there was, of course, less potential to pour these energies into political reform and there is doubtless validity in the assertion that 'the excessive interest in the arts must be regarded as over compensation for this enforced political passivity'.[6]

The legitimacy, authenticity and even mythology of the Golden Age has been so much debated in Denmark that some feel the term now has little currency.[7] But the folklore and stereotypes surrounding the concept are at heart authentic. The names of the writer Hans Christian Andersen and the philosopher Søren Kierkegaard may be the most famous beyond Denmark's geographical and temporal boundaries, but others, if lesser known, are no less illustrious or worthy. These might include the internationally renowned sculptor Bertel Thorvaldsen; the influential theologian, poet, philologist and historian N.F.S. Grundtvig; B.S. Ingemann, who wrote historical novels inspired by Sir Walter Scott; Steen Steensen Blicher whose short stories gave a voice to everyday folk and their milieu; the romantic lyric poet and playwright Adam Oehlenschläger; or the choreographer and founder of modern ballet August Bournonville. They, and others, helped Denmark emulate classical Athens in spawning within a few decades enough talent and original thought to occupy commentators for centuries.

For a non-Danish audience the close intersections between all branches of creative enterprise at this time can be bewildering. A figure such as the physicist and chemist Hans Christian Ørsted is perhaps a key to approaching the triumphs of this period, being an exceptionally gifted, yet wholly characteristic, product of the age. The discoverer of electro-magnetism (in 1820) and a tireless proponent of natural philosophy, Ørsted was a man of immense and diverse achievements. He excelled in his own disciplines, was in intellectual discourse with everybody of note in all fields of human endeavour (including his fiercest detractors) and straddled the entire panoply of Golden Age enterprise. He was not merely a world leader in his own fields, but somebody who widely concerned himself with the arts and who also composed poetry. Before modern science made such notions seem mildly ridiculous, he held avidly to a belief, which he expressed lucidly, in the interdependence and coexistence of art and science. He saw these as complementary facets of the divine order that ran through both rational and emotional thought, and through empirical discipline and spiritual speculation. Ørsted was not alone in propounding a view that both nature and the work of art are manifestations of a divine reason, and that the artist is therefore the instrument of God's articulation of the underlying harmony of our world. Viewed in this light, scientific romanticism, or natural romanticism as it was also labelled, was not considered a contradiction in terms. Rather it was to Golden Age minds a palpable reality wherein everything existed under the auspices of a divine order, the existence of which might be glimpsed, verified and celebrated via the various and interconnected fields of human enterprise.[8]

This was first and foremost, then, an age for the polymath, the entrepreneur and the psychologically adroit. And it was through this tumultuous period of intense intellectual commotion and breathtaking accomplishment that the unlikely figure of Christen Købke ambled: a man of few words, uncertain direction, little introspection and even less reading – an unassuming individual of domestic habits, diffident and humble to a fault, given to religious doubts that oscillated between devout piety and the mildest of religious petulance, and whose closest brush with the romantic maelstrom of existential angst was his self-documented martyrdom to recurrent indigestion[1]. Købke, who struggled economically, who failed to gain membership of the Academy, and whose reputation amounted to little more than the approbation of the small artistic community of Copenhagen and the inner circles of friends and family, would have been dumbfounded could he have known that this period of the nation's supreme cultural flowering would also come to be labelled 'the Age of Købke.'[9] Even less could he have imagined that he would be fêted by posterity as 'the best Danish painter of the period', 'the supreme Golden Age painter' or 'the most outstanding Danish painter of the Golden Age.'[10] Yet such is the case. Købke's disarmingly simple but refined output, his precise and clear-cut manner, sharp focus and pristine light are now regarded as synonymous with the age. He remains unrivalled in his ability to invest the simplest corner of nature or town with charm and delicacy, eschewing rhetoric in a manner that seems quintessentially modern. It is as if his small, uneventful scenes, devoid of narrative, presage a methodology in which light, composition, colour and form become ends in themselves.

Købke's background and character, however, as well as what he achieved in a brief lifetime, make him an unlikely standard bearer for an age of cultural triumph. At first glance his greatest affinity with the period seems to be the simple one that his life (1810–1848) coincided almost exactly with the Golden Age, which begins with the nation's post-Napoleonic resurrection, and ends with the abolition of autocracy and the establishment of parliamentary democracy in 1849. In this respect Købke is situated securely within the confines of the era and can speak for this period alone. The wonder of the age might be expressed simply in this way: how did a small, defeated nation whose intellectual life existed almost solely within Copenhagen, ruled by an intolerant absolutist monarchy, generate such diverse cultural riches? Similarly, of Købke's contribution it might be asked: how did an artist of sedate temperament, lacking the dramatic peaks and troughs of traditional genius, whose key works span less than a decade, who achieved little recognition in his day and who focused consistently on small, intimate and prosaic subjects, come to be hailed as the paradigm of Golden Age art?

The term Golden Age, or 'guldalderen', was a literary epithet not coined until 1890 by the Danish critic Valdemar Vedel. However, the polymath Ørsted was as prescient of later concerns over this terminology as he was unassuming when he wrote to the poet

5 · *Portrait of the Artist's Father, Master Baker Peter Berendt Købke*, c.1835
Statens Museum for Kunst, Copenhagen

Oehlenschläger of 'the stupid conceit with which so many writers would like to turn our day and age into a *golden age*'.[11] Despite the praise subsequently heaped upon the achievements of the period, its chief characteristics were a self-effacing modesty and lack of pretension, qualities which allow Købke to be seen as its ideal representative.

In all contemporary accounts of the artist, and through his own letters, we are faced with a man of avowedly limited intellectual pretensions, but of immense honesty, integrity and candour. He was an ingenuous person, naïve in the best sense of that word, without guile or malice, a sincere and immensely 'likeable' character, a person on whom the evils of the world could find neither nourishment nor purchase. Emil Hannover, in 1893 the first art historian to write a monograph on Købke, characterised him as childlike and averred that he 'cultivated the ability to see at the expense of all other abilities'.[12] He continued less charitably:

> He was born without any creative imagination, and he lacked the acumen to cobble together anything ingenious. He was empty and barren as soon as he closed his eyes and sought to imagine a picture without having the natural scene before him. That is what he was like in his youth, and that is what he continued to be like.[13]

In one sense this is rather negative, but Hannover also believed that Købke possessed a childlike simplicity and frankness that allowed him to scrutinise natural phenomena with unparalleled clarity. And the assertion is not without foundation: Købke was a superlative artist, not a writer. Indeed, his letters are idiosyncratic in spelling and punctuation, lacking in intellectual revelation, frequently devout and humble, but sincere and lively, with the personality described by his contemporaries strongly present.[14] But he is also an elusive personality who rarely gives us much insight into the deeper recesses of his thought processes and to a large extent he remains an enigma.

Købke had an unremarkable upbringing. From a prosperous family, he was the fifth of eleven children (five girls and six boys) born to Peter [5] and Cecilia Købke [4]. Peter was a successful baker, as was his father before him, and despite the setback of the British bombardment of 1807 (the enterprising Peter set up ovens in the garden until repairs to the bakery were carried out), the Købkes maintained an affluent lifestyle. Peter and Cecilia were by all accounts a close and hardworking couple. They were also cousins, a pattern of intermarrying that Købke would later follow when in 1837 he married his cousin Susanne Cecilie Købke, or 'Sanne' as he called her [51].[15] Life in the Købke extended family household was lively and warm and at various times, even into adulthood, sons and daughters of disparate ages (there was a ten-year gap between the oldest and youngest children) lived together under the same roof. Sometimes, as it would be in Købke's case, this arrangement included partners (who were often relatives) and children, and the atmosphere was one of boisterous conviviality. The fulcrum of the household was Peter, a redoubtable but amiable presence whom Købke is said to have idolised. Certainly he was close to his father, portrayed him on numerous occasions, was his frequent walking companion, and in his letters repeatedly expressed a care for his health. Moreover, his father appreciated Købke's talent and placed no obstacles in his pursuit of a career as a painter, a situation not common in the lives of artists. In time Købke and his own wife and family would rely heavily on Peter's kindness in providing a roof over their heads, and it seems that he never begrudged them a generous share of the financial stability that his son failed to secure as a painter.

After the British bombardment of his premises, Peter sold up and tried his luck as a brewer, before returning to baking in Hillerød, close to the castle of Frederiksborg where

6 · Apart from his two-year journey to Italy, Købke's life was spent mainly in the areas marked on this map of Copenhagen, dated 1844.

A. *The Citadel: home to the Købke family from 1819 until 1833.*

B. *Toldbodvej: Købke shared a studio here with his friend the landscape painter Frederik Sødring.*

C. *The Royal Danish Academy of Fine Arts at Charlottenborg Palace: Købke was a student at the Academy from 1822 until 1833.*

D. *The Sortedam Lake and Blegdammen: the family moved from the Citadel to the large house at Blegdammen where Købke lived with his parents from 1833 until 1845.*

E. *Frederiksborggade: Købke lived here with his wife and children from 1845 until his death in 1848.*

Map reproduced by kind permission of The Royal Library, Copenhagen.

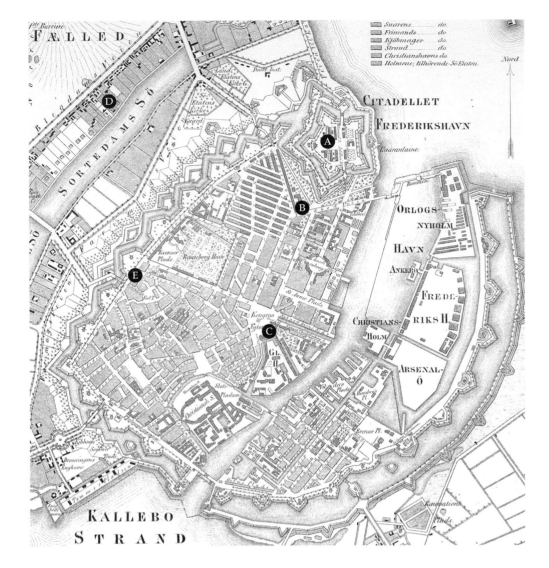

Købke would later find painterly inspiration in the 1830s. In 1818 Peter accepted a lucrative fifteen-year contract as master baker to the military Citadel in Copenhagen, just outside the city ramparts, and the following year the family moved there. This secured the family's prosperity, since the contract was to a guaranteed clientele. The limits of this self-contained community, which was home to Købke from the ages of roughly nine to twenty-three, perhaps suited his temperament. A sickly child, most accounts state that he took up drawing to pass time during bouts of illness which would plague him throughout his life. As the son of a middle-class family he was taught at home by a private tutor, but, since he began his tutelage at the Royal Danish Academy of Fine Arts at an early age, it can be assumed that he must have had a proclivity towards the visual arts from childhood. He remained closest to his sisters, to whom the majority of his surviving letters to family are addressed, and a prevailing mood of domesticity certainly pervades his temperament. In addition to this, a sense of insularity characterises aspects of both Købke's life and art. His thirty-seven years were lived within Copenhagen and its environs, firstly in the Citadel, and, from 1833, still with his parents, at Blegdammen near Lake Sortedam, a rural location outside the city ramparts, but within walking distance of the city centre. After his father's death in 1843, Købke, Sanne and their children moved back within the city proper in 1845, and since the artist's education took place at the Academy in the Charlottenborg Palace, close to the

7 · P.C. Skovgaard,
*Portrait of Christen Købke, c.*1846
Århus Kunstmuseum

Citadel, by the time of his death in 1848 Købke had seldom moved out of the compass of the city or its closest outskirts [6].

This apparent insularity also conditions the distinctive phases of his art, which, with little overlap, correspond to the chronology of his life, and which provide the structure for the sections that follow: the artist's days as a student and early influences at Charlottenborg; his life and works in the Citadel; painting trips to Frederiksborg during the 1830s; the move to Blegdammen; his reluctant visit to Italy from 1838 to 1840, and his subsequent return to Denmark. Throughout his life Købke produced an astounding body of portraits, which will be considered separately, but the most distinctive characteristic of his art and personality is his attachment to locations close at hand, and to atmospheres with which he is familiar – what would now be termed his 'comfort zone'.

A creative self-sufficiency and contentment must be inferred from this, but if it speaks of a conservative nature his output from this limited range of resources was rich and prodigious. Occasionally he ventured further afield: to the countryside of Zealand to visit family members, to Jutland to stay with friends and family, and eventually to Italy which was considered essential for an aspiring artist. In general, however, he lived an unassuming existence absorbed in painting, about which he did not theorise or proselytise, and lacked any of the romantic unruliness sometimes associated with the artistic temperament. As an illustration of this it is often asserted that Købke was careful whilst painting and sketching to ensure he was always close enough to be home for dinner.[16] When striking out as far as Frederiksborg he was assured of the hospitality of his sister Conradine, who lived in nearby Hillerød, and even in Rome he managed to breakfast regularly with his sister Sophie and her husband, the artist F.C. Krohn.[17] He probably had good reasons for ensuring the quality and regularity of his meals, as would anybody with health problems stemming from a dietary disorder (we glimpse as much from his letters). Købke therefore could hardly be more the antithesis of Kierkegaard's conviction that 'Geniuses are like thunder-storms: they run against the wind, terrify people, cleanse the air.'[18]

But if Købke's circumstances seem claustrophobic, they were not radically different from the experience of the age. Artists worked chiefly within the confined spaces of the city and its fringes, seeking their inspiration largely from everyday life and suffering together from the same limited range of patronage. Unlike the magnificent example of Thorvaldsen, who spent nearly all of his life in Italy in the pay of the Vatican and the European aristocracy, for artists in Denmark economic revival and the emergence of a mercantile patronage was slow. The Academy and court provided too few opportunities for work and private collecting was sparse. The establishment in 1825 by Eckersberg of the Fine Arts Society (Kunstforeningen) gave painters an alternative to selling and exhibiting, and most crucially supported them through the period following national bankruptcy. A private organisation promoting art within middle-class, moneyed circles, it helped secure the acceptance of national themes and worked in an ingeniously commercial manner, commissioning works which were then raffled off to a lucky winner. Købke was to benefit from its patronage in a career otherwise blighted by the lack of outlets for professional artists. But again, in this he was not alone, merely working as others under the constraints of the age.[19]

It has often been noted that Copenhagen's ramparts enclosed a community, where everybody knew everybody else (and, as in Købke's case, were frequently intermarried). Despite the parochial associations this might evoke, the intellectual fecundity of the Golden Age can be seen as a cultural retort, a laboratory of concentrated interactivity and experimentation – of what is now termed interdisciplinarity – and where the currency of creative reciprocity travelled swiftly. It was against this backdrop of innovative intellectual turbulence and unparalleled debate concerning the nation's character and direction, that the unlikely figure of the master baker's son, Christen Schjellerup Købke, took his first steps towards engagement with Danish artistic culture, as he entered the Royal Danish Academy of Fine Arts in 1822, aged eleven.

Charlottenborg

The Royal Danish Academy of Fine Arts, housed (as it still is) in the Charlottenborg Palace, a short walk from Købke's home in the Citadel, was an august institution. Founded by Frederik V in 1754 it was, like many of its European counterparts, long dominated by Italian Renaissance models, and had no distinct national identity. There had been very few notable painters of Danish origin, and foreign artists were imported by the court and foreign professors taught at the Academy. A generation later, however, in the 1780s, most of these posts were held by Danes, and indigenous talents were coming to the fore. Nicolai Abildgaard and Jens Juel were amongst the earliest Danish painters whose works could bear comparison with their European counterparts, but what they painted tended still to be standard academic fare, with sources rooted in the Bible and antiquity, and done in a neoclassical style. The results of these high-minded but conservative endeavours were displayed at the annual spring exhibitions in Charlottenborg. Rather like other European academies, these exhibitions acted as a shop window for establishing reputations and acquiring commissions, but they also set the standard against which young, aspiring artists could model and judge their own progress.

When Købke entered the Academy in May 1822, aged just eleven, having passed a rudimentary entrance examination, he did so at an opportune time, as significant changes to the structure and curriculum were beginning to revitalise Danish art. It was against this background that his outlook was formed and his talent fostered. Initially, however, he was placed on the traditional treadmill of learning by rote. In common with all students he advanced slowly through a routine of drawing objects and parts of the body, and it was not until 1827, five years into his studies, that he progressed to copying from classical casts, and, later that year, working in the life class. Clearly his entry at so young an age gave him time to mature and develop slowly under this exacting but systematic training which, if nothing else, produced draughtsmen of breathtaking ability. It was not unusual, however, for students to start so early. Of Købke's renowned contemporaries, Johan Thomas Lundbye entered the Academy at fifteen, Constantin Hansen at twelve and Wilhelm Marstrand at sixteen.[20]

In part the sheer youth of many of the students emphasised the fact that this was a long and arduous training process, more akin to an apprenticeship than a process of nurturing creative talents. Indeed, the Academy additionally functioned as a technical school, and tuition in the fine arts was supplemented by classes in drawing and ornamentation for apprentices working in the decorative art industries. In 1828, for instance, six years after Købke's arrival, the number of students attending the Academy was 500, of whom 300 were apprentices – the latter having, it seems, a bad reputation for public unruliness.[21]

Traditionally, education at the Academy had been haphazard, with student attendance largely voluntary and classes not being given on a regular daily basis. Studio instruction took place in the evenings, from five until eight, and was supplemented by private supervision in the professors' studios for the most talented. The main curriculum consisted of classes in mathematics, theory of perspective, anatomy, history, art history and mythology, supported by access to the Academy's library. It was necessary to pass tests to advance to each level, the most important of which was a test in general knowledge before students were permitted to draw from the nude model.[22] If, later, they wished to enter the competition for the gold medal, the highest award given at the Academy, students had also to sit an exam related to the full scope of their lectures. For whatever reason, Købke chose not to enter the gold medal competition.

Nonetheless, the Academy attracted some significant talents and in time was favoured by many foreign artists. The German romantic painters Caspar David Friedrich and Georg Friedrich Kersting both studied there, as did the Norwegian landscape painter Johan Christian Dahl. Friedrich and Dahl, who, from 1823 shared a house in Dresden, continued to exhibit at the the Academy spring exhibitions and their differing influences infiltrated Danish art, particularly from the 1840s onwards. Also at the Academy briefly, between 1799 and 1800, was the German romantic and mystic painter Philip Otto Runge. He was not, however, impressed by the training he received, nor by his fellow students. In a letter home Runge complained of the students' lack of intellectual interests and tendency to waste their evenings playing cards. He confirmed also the appalling behaviour of the apprentices.[23]

During Købke's time at the Academy such significant changes occurred that it could legitimately be described as 'the equal of that in Paris and superior to that in Rome', or,

9 · Wilhelm Bendz, *The Life Class at The Royal Academy of Fine Arts*, 1826 Statens Museum for Kunst, Copenhagen

even more audaciously, as 'the most progressive art Academy in Europe.'[24] This turnaround was due chiefly to the efforts of C.W. Eckersberg and his colleague J.L. Lund, who were jointly appointed as professors in 1818. Together they set about revitalising an institution in dire need of reform and Eckersberg's influence in particular was to prove the catalyst to Købke's development into an artist of immense stature.

Initially, however, Købke entered the studio of the eighty-year-old C.A. Lorentzen, who, although remembered now as a pedestrian and uninspiring artist, gave Købke a thorough technical and formal grounding and with whom the equable youth appears to have shared a warm and reciprocal relationship. Lorentzen, along with his colleagues Abildgaard and Juel, had also tutored Friedrich and Runge. Thus, after many years of diligent copying in preparation for studio instruction, Købke began his training proper in 1826, in safe if not inspiring hands.

It is tempting to conjecture along which lines Købke's talent might have developed had he remained under Lorentzen, but in May 1828 the elderly artist, who could recall the Academy's eighteenth-century inception, died and Købke was admitted in June of that year to Eckersberg's studio, the professor marking this momentous event in his diary with the laconic comment: 'Promised Købke the baker I would accept his son for tuition.'[25] Here Købke did not merely thrive but positively flourished. Even the most rudimentary review of his work during this time shows an artist making a quantum leap from proficiency to excellence as the quality of his painting moves into a different dimension.

In Købke's day the changes wrought by Eckersberg and Lund were not chiefly to the intellectual syllabus, although this did improve. In 1819 the archaeologist Finn Magnusen held his first lecture on Nordic mythology, and in 1829 N.L. Høyen was appointed as a professor, also lecturing on Nordic mythology. Høyen was to be a vastly influential figure in Danish art and a powerful proponent of a nationally-based culture. For the students, however, the real revolution was to the practical tuition, largely due to Eckersberg, who instilled his students with a devotion to truth to nature and working directly from life.

It was under Eckersberg and Lund that academic pupils began working from the live

10 · *Eckersberg and Marstrand on a Study Excursion*, 1832
Department of Prints and Drawings, Statens Museum for Kunst, Copenhagen

model. Both had long championed figure painting, introducing the discipline of working from the male nude in 1824 and from the female nude from 1833. Wilhelm Bendz's painting of this period, *The Life Class at the Royal Academy of Fine Arts* [9], produced the year Købke entered Lorentzen's studio gives a fascinating insight into the practicalities of the regular evening sessions where Købke would have drawn the male nude by artificial light. Bendz has already assimilated the modern exhortation to engage with everyday reality, here turning the ordinary processes of artistic training into art, producing not only an intriguing period document but also a meditation on the process of making art.[26]

Painting in this manner, by artificial illumination, was traditionally employed to ensure unvarying and consistent light, but the results lacked naturalness, tending instead to the theatrical. In the search for greater artistic truth Eckersberg introduced the practice of painting the nude by natural light, but, more audaciously, in 1822 he had instigated a summer course where students were instructed to paint not merely in natural light, but outdoors.[27] The inclusion in the curriculum of study excursions around the Copenhagen environs was unprecedented. Indeed, it is asserted that 'No other professor of any academy in Europe allowed this kind of open-air painting to form an essential part of the training of young artists.'[28] Købke has left us a charming drawing [10] of one such outing, and he clearly flourished under this liberal regime. In a journal entry for 27 May 1831, characteristic of his earnest piety, he notes: ' … with the good Prof. Eckersb. and all of us his children for a drive to Frederiksdal, and enjoyed ourselves extremely. God grant that I may experience many suchlike days with wealth of learning, and always continue on the Path of Truth, and that I will become a good and useful man.'[29]

Eckersberg's appeal as an artist and his qualities as a reforming and progressive teacher deserve closer scrutiny, since it is from his influence that the foundations of Danish Golden Age painting took shape. He studied initially under Abildgaard before visiting Paris in 1811, where he was taught by Jacques-Louis David, who recognised and encouraged his talent. From here Eckersberg moved to Rome in 1813, where the major breakthrough in his art occurred. Equipping himself with a stool and portable paint box he set about recording the Eternal City in a series of breathtakingly realistic, yet curiously fragmented, sketches. Whilst the practise of open-air painting was not in itself new (Pierre-Henri de Valenciennes and Thomas Jones had pioneered the method in Rome and Naples respectively in the late eighteenth century) Eckersberg's productions were neither spontaneous painterly exercises, nor part of a progression leading to a finished work. The extent to which these pieces, small enough to fit within the lid of the portable paint box, were completed in situ cannot be fully ascertained, but they have a freshness and immediacy which places them in a class of their own and illustrate Eckersberg's idiosyncratic take on subjects so familiar it might be thought there was nothing new to be derived from them.[30] The importance of these works and the influence they were to have resides in their bearing the hallmarks of what would become the major characteristics of Danish Golden Age art. They are closely observed, detailed, disarmingly natural, yet set in an idealised, tranquil light that lends the scene a curious mixture of stillness and astonishing realism, rather as if time has been suspended. Eckersberg recorded once that as a boy he chanced to see a cityscape reflected in a black bottle on a summer's day and that in this he saw the scene in miniature as a perfect painting. This was a way of seeing that permeated his mature works and which came to fruition in Rome where he produced sharply detailed and precise observations from life that treated subject matter of significant cultural or historical resonance in an entirely unassuming manner [11].

Eckersberg retained the harmonious proportions of monumental buildings within his tiny paintings, and though scaling reality down he sacrificed nothing of his normal visual range; even the largest vistas could be contained within the smallest of canvases. Yet, there

11 · C.W. Eckersberg,
View of the Via Sacra, Rome, 1814
Ny Carlsberg Glyptotek, Copenhagen

12 · C.W. Eckersberg,
Roman Courtyard, 1813–16
Ribe Kunstmuseum

is also something radically dispassionate about these works that have a feel of what could be termed a photographic vision, possibly the outcome of using a lens in the form of a perspective-octant, which creates the impression of a scene chosen casually. This was Eckersberg's own invention, a portable device similar to Dürer's drawing machine, that fixed the artist's sight-line at a set distance from a wooden frame divided into squares by a lattice of wires, through which he could plot and transfer precisely to his canvas or paper what it encompassed.[31]

Like the viewfinder on a modern camera, it fixed the image to be copied, but, as with a camera, the result could appear emotionally detached. Eckersberg's approach was often likened, not always approvingly, to that of a mechanistic and indiscriminate eye, which took in and faithfully reproduced both the essential and the banal. All of these traits are exemplified in a small work depicting a courtyard in an unidentified location [12].By comparison with Eckersberg's Roman views, it strikes a prosaic note, yet it attains its objectives, in meticulously recording a specific place, right down to the decrepit masonry and the peeling and damp-discoloured plasterwork.

A modernity of approach certainly resides in Eckersberg's direct and democratic observation, which has been summed up thus: 'It was clearly Eckersberg who chose the views, not the other way around.'[32] Put simply, Eckersberg led rather than followed, and his Roman works are the antithesis of the prevailing academic hierarchy of subject matter, informed by precedent rather than observation. This took Danish art towards a fresher and more innovative position, but the acceptance of this way of working was effected by Eckersberg only after he took up his professorship at the Academy in 1818. An inspiring teacher who led by example, Eckersberg's influence has rightly meant that he has come to be regarded as a father figure in Danish art. Whilst his Roman *vedute* were not the foundation of his reputation (he also painted large-scale history works, portraits, and was fascinated by marine scenes) they were to influence a generation of students, including Købke, who had the opportunity to see Eckersberg's Roman views which hung in the 'yellow room' of his studio apartment. They helped to lay the foundations of modern Danish art with their insistence on attaining the ideal through the real. A believer in the grammar of art, Eckersberg published two books on perspective and kept meticulous meteorological records to further his comprehension of the natural world. He similarly exhorted his students to 'examine the great book of nature' so that pictures might approximate to the real world. However, the goal was not only to fix the motif, but also to reach a greater appreciation of the underlying ideal, or 'fundamental image' that emanated from its divine source.[33] The objective was not realism, but truth and, to attain this objective, artists were encouraged to seek the eternal in the mundane, and so long as they painted well, to paint anything: '... paint from nature, no matter what it might be, farmhouses, churches, castles, trees, plants or animals, in short whatever is there'.[34]

Eckersberg's students responded willingly to this unorthodox but appealing proposal. Frederik Sødring's small view, *The Rear Courtyard of Charlottenborg Palace* [13], is a perfect example of Eckersberg's Roman practices transferred to Copenhagen – a 'modern' subject and an attempt to record in precise detail a simple scene close to hand. Sødring has taken Eckersberg's injunction to heart by stepping into the nearest courtyard adjoining Charlottenborg. The laundry might even be Eckersberg's (his apartment is just above the porch). The whole seems merely an exercise in the observation of shifting light and its effect on textures: brick, cobbles, wooden tubs, the moss-covered porch roof, and the play of sunlight and shadow. The subject is clearly mundane, but that the artist felt comfortable with such a lowly scene is characteristic of Eckersberg's exhortation towards modest contemporary subject matter treated with the utmost fidelity.

This mixture of 'scientific' examination and an underlying idealism that art might in some manner address the divinely harmonious nature of the world, even its most ordinary corners, was not Eckersberg's preserve, but was more widely a fundamental attribute of Golden Age endeavour. In the fine arts, however, it found its outlet largely through Eckersberg's example, and then through his progressive teaching methods, to which his students were indebted.

13 · Frederik Sødring, *The Rear Courtyard of Charlottenborg Palace*, 1828
Statens Museum for Kunst, Copenhagen

14 · *View from a Window in Eckersberg's Studio of a Wing in Charlottenborg, c.1829*
Ny Carlsberg Glyptotek, Copenhagen

15 · *Nude Figure. Sitting Boy*, 1833
Statens Museum for Kunst, Copenhagen

Købke in particular benefited greatly from Eckersberg's tutelage. His example of working from nature was to be a practice Købke would embrace as he pursued his artistic aims around his home in the Citadel. His *View from a Window in Eckersberg's Studio of a Wing in Charlottenborg* [14], executed when he was only nineteen, shows a degree of naivety in the way he has treated the figures, but there is a thorough engagement with Eckersberg's stringent perspective and his injunction to paint from everyday life. Købke has simply looked out from his master's studio and caught the moment in all its accidental, truncated detail. There are also, as in Eckersberg's Roman works, glimpses of places within the principal view – here the brightly lit buildings receding down the west side of the present day Bredgade. At the same time he has caught the sense of freshness of light and air, of crisp, clear and convincing atmosphere that characterises Eckersberg's best works. From this point on there is a fundamental transformation of Købke's art from one of conventional competency to that of an assured and proficient talent playing to his undoubted strengths of precise observation and aesthetic subtlety, the credit for which surely rests with Eckersberg.

Købke concluded his formal training around 1832–3 but continued to study informally with Eckersberg until 1834–5, particularly from the live model. Købke's works of this kind show a marked degree of informality and lack of the usual academic rhetoric. Where customarily the nude male was studied for inclusion in history paintings, Købke emphasises the everyday nature of the sitters, frequently drawn from the nearby Citadel guards or the sailors of Nyhavn, with their period whiskers, rubicund cheeks and the sunburnt arms of outdoor workers [16]. They are nevertheless graceful in their artless poses, placed in

16 · *Male Nude*, 1833
The Royal Danish Academy of Fine Arts, Copenhagen

17 · Henry Fuseli, *The Artist Sunk in Despair at the Grandeur of Classical Fragments*, 1778–80
Kunsthaus, Zurich

empty Academy rooms with just a box for support. *Male Nude* and *Nude Figure. Sitting Boy* [15], two works painted just months apart in 1833, show Købke's continuing ties with Eckersberg beyond his student days, which had culminated with his debut at the spring exhibition in Charlottenborg in 1831. Here he exhibited four paintings that in the maturity of their conception gave notice of the arrival of a major talent: *The Transept of Århus Cathedral* [31]; *View of the Plaster Cast Collection at Charlottenborg* [8]; *Cigar Seller at the Northern Exit from the Citadel* [26]; and *View of the Square in the Citadel Looking towards the Citadel Ramparts* [20].[35] All are images of contemporary, Danish life emanating from Eckersberg's precepts of direct observation from nature and of seeking the ideal in the mundanity of one's immediate surroundings.

Købke did not seek the prestigious gold medal that was the focus of artistic ambition in the Academy's career ladder. Possibly a lack of the inventiveness required to conceptualise a work of history, without recourse to direct visual observation, deterred him. But it might equally indicate that he had no inclination towards becoming a history painter and had already, through Eckersberg's example, found the proper focus of his vocation.[36]

The closest Købke came to addressing the weighty issues of antiquity was an image of a male figure absorbed in consideration of part of the Academy's cast collection [8]. The work might infer a meditation on the ideal, which still, in contemporary Copenhagen, was the goal of creative achievement. The works on display are all identifiable, including the river god Illisos from the west pediment of the Parthenon and a single metope (the rectangular architectural element from a Doric frieze) from its south side, arranged above Thorvaldsen's copy of the head of one of the Dioscuri (in mythology the twins Castor and Pollux) from Rome's Piazza Quirinale.[37] The scope of these casts speaks also of a change in fashion away from the more mannered models of the Hellenistic age to the supposed integrity of the classical period and in particular to the work of Phidias, the greatest of classical sculptors and to whom the Parthenon decorations are credited. In 1828 Eckersberg had reorganised the cast collection along these lines, an event celebrated that November with a torchlight viewing, at which Købke was present.[38]

The refinement and subtlety of the painting is evidence of a painter, still only twenty years of age, working now at the highest level of aesthetic accomplishment. A Købke trademark is what might be termed the symphonic blending of colour harmonies. Typically this is done through significant but muted tones (here of grey and white) which are sharply offset by a darker complementary (the man's black apparel) and then enlivened by a single note of a purer colour – here the yellow duster.

And yet despite the virtuoso skill on display, the work is still a curious and unconventionally matter-of-fact contemplation on the classical world. In tone and treatment it is a world away from more usually romantic considerations of the lost glory and faded grandeur of civilisations past, most famously encapsulated in Fuseli's image of the artist mourning the demise of antiquity and his own inability to measure up to its unrivalled standards [17]. Where Fuseli both monumentalises the products of the past and amplifies the emotion they generate, Købke somehow reduces these enduring masterpieces to passive if beautiful objects which inspire only quiet inspection. The fact that some of the ancient pieces he chose to include are headless may be intentional, a comment perhaps on the fragmentary nature of the sources. The work also suggests that for Købke the cast class was not a moribund activity, but represented aesthetic principles that were still valid. The painting is a sincere yet unpretentious homage to the ancient world, but one sited firmly in the ordinary activities of the present.

The Citadel ⤳

18 · Detail from *The Northern Drawbridge to the Citadel in Copenhagen*, 1837 [28]

The National Gallery, London

Other than the works produced during his academic studies, Købke's main body of paintings at this time concern the Citadel, which was home to the artist and his family from 1819 to 1833. A self-contained world which remains largely unchanged today [19], the Citadel was situated in countryside outside the city ramparts. A military fort, shaped as a pentagram and surrounded by moats and ramparts, it housed around 600 soldiers and their families and maintained its own church, mill, forge and bakery. Bordered by land on all sides except to the east, where the Øresund gives access across the sea to Sweden, it held little strategic importance after Denmark's military humiliations, its fortifications being long covered over with grass and trees. It had too its sinister aspect, being home also to a large contingent of convicts (known as 'slaves') who acted as forced labour. By all accounts a lawless and insanitary pigsty, it would be hard to deduce this from Købke's bright and airy paintings of a place he knew in intimate detail.[39]

The sole exception to the otherwise sunny and cheerful images he painted at this time is his *View of the Square in the Citadel Looking towards the Citadel Ramparts* [20]. The painting contains identifiable characters and a narrative element: Major J.J. Krohn gives orders to a Sergeant Sporch, in charge of the 'slaves', as Købke's father looks on. Peter Købke's bakery business had premises in both North and South Storehouses, which flanked the large and impressive parade ground in front of the Citadel church. The family resided in the North Storehouse, from where this work was painted. Købke's viewpoint is from inside his own home, looking across to his father's bakery, the buttressed building on the right, within which the glow of the ovens can just be discerned. In some ways it is an awkward work, though the nuances of light and shade are sensitively rendered. Yet it also strikes an unusually darker chord, both in the tiny figure walking spectre-like across the ramparts, and a detail not immediately obvious: the figure operating the pump is shackled – and may be working for Købke's father. There is ultimately as much shadow as light in a work that suggests an awareness by the artist that his cosy everyday surroundings had a bleaker connotation. Yet, two concurrent works featuring the bakery create very different impressions.

View of the Courtyard near the Bakery in the Citadel [21] is an earthbound, yet aesthetically satisfying work which merges a stunning variety of detail, textures and light effects into a harmonious whole. The mood is fresh, the azure sky acting as a counter to the shady courtyard, with the red roof of a building on the other side of the wooden fence providing a note of strong colour. The unbridled horses suggest repose and the diminutive figures of two children, on the ramparts above the red-tiled roof, add a playful note. Despite the semblance of a rural setting, the verdant landscape beyond the fence is the Citadel fortifications and Købke exploits this contrast to the full, producing a work that portrays a business environment in the language of a rural idyll. Minute details add to the work's sense of hyper-reality, including a series of dewy cobwebs on the fence. On the extreme right, seemingly included by accident, is a narrow section of wall that frames the limits of the view, but suggests the continuance of a real world beyond this. Købke would often employ this simple but effective device to abruptly cut and frame his works, suggesting that this is an ostensibly random view, which is at odds, of course, with the careful realisation of his painting. Although one of Købke's smallest and most daringly simple works, it is without doubt one of his most accomplished, illustrating how the lessons at Charlottenborg were still nurturing his artistic development. *View from the Loft of the Grain Store at the Bakery in the Citadel* [22] presents an even more idyllic vision observed from within a

dark, high interior, out towards the sunny grounds of the Citadel. Again, what might be mistaken for countryside are the Citadel ramparts, but the effect is of a pastorale. Købke depicts his sister Grethe (Cecilie Margrethe) absorbed in knitting, walking up the wooden ramp, oblivious of our gaze but watched by two young boys. A tiny detail in this painting, seemingly not remarked on before, is the little spherical object hanging on Grethe's right wrist, securing her wool – a device that allowed women to continue their knitting whilst strolling. This adds a note of industry to the scene but simultaneously identifies the gentility of the figure since such items, made of wood or sometimes silver, were indicative of the wealthier middle class.[40]

Købke regarded this as an important work as, contrary to usual practice, he made preparatory drawings for it. The result is an exquisitely structured image of a mathematical complexity born of Eckersberg's insistence on the mastery of perspective. Like Eckersberg's *Roman Courtyard*, it manages to appear totally artless despite its intricate underpinning. It is also a painting that illustrates Købke's masterly handling of light. The dim interior is infiltrated by sunlight, which harmonises with the exterior, taken up largely by the dark mass of the tree, but relieved by the light that seeps between its leaves. The light simultaneously catches the edges of Grethe's dress and shoulders, and illuminates the view to the horizon. What at first glance appears a dichotomy between interior and exterior, is in fact a complementary and sublimely conceived image: the cool attic is warmed by the sun, but the

19 · Photograph of the present-day Citadel showing the ramparts, houses and moat.

20 · *View of the Square in the Citadel Looking towards the Citadel Ramparts*, c.1831 National Gallery of Scotland, Edinburgh

21 · *View of the Courtyard near the Bakery in the Citadel, c.*1832
Ny Carlsberg Glyptotek, Copenhagen

22 · *View from the Loft of the Grain Store at the Bakery in the Citadel,* 1831
Statens Museum for Kunst, Copenhagen

23 · *View of the Citadel Ramparts towards Langelinie and the Naval Harbour, c.1832*
Statens Museum for Kunst, Copenhagen

24 · *View from the Citadel Ramparts across the Moat and Langelinie towards the Limekiln, c.*1833
Ordrupgaard, Copenhagen

bright exterior offers shade. The colour scheme is similar to that employed in the painting of the bakery courtyard and characteristic of Købke's work at this time: earth-coloured harmonies offset by a stronger hue – here the coral dress. Within the painting's borders, Købke employs yet another framing device (the loft door) which in turn is bisected by the partially glimpsed horizon.[41] This is an exceedingly subtle and nuanced work born of an exceptional pictorial sensibility and it serves to illustrate that a lack of sophistication in his writing was not a bar to the artist expressing himself visually in the most eloquent manner.

These and several small landscapes of the period show Købke working within the constraints of an enclosed space, and seeking the unfamiliar in familiar surroundings, all facets of Eckersberg's teaching. *View of the Citadel Ramparts towards Langelinie and the Naval Harbour* [23] shows a section of the winding inner rampart, looking across the moat and over the outer wall. Perched in between is a guardhouse and sundry buildings, and in the distance a harbour is indicated by a forest of masts. The major area of this canvas, however, is sky, the accurate rendering of which was a preoccupation he shared with Eckersberg. This small canvas has the depth and space of a wide vista, expertly controlled by an artifice that seems effortless, but is the result of Købke's diligent observation and prolonged labour. Treating the same theme in *View from the Citadel Ramparts across the Moat and Langelinie towards the Limekiln* [24], Købke manages a wholly different perspective. This, the only work of its kind that he exhibited at Charlottenborg, has a tighter finish and more romantic lighting, and he boldly divides the lower section of the canvas vertically – one half occupied by the rampart, the other by the moat and a view further afield. The wonderful evocation of a still summer's day is a poetic image forged from the most mundane contemporary material. And whilst, like Eckersberg, Købke was occasionally censured for his apparent lack of discrimination when selecting his subjects, a modern audience more easily delights in his obvious care for light, colour, air and compositional experimentation. These landscapes were not done in preparation for more finished productions, nor are they impromptu sketches, but highly specific renderings of time and place. Emil Hannover described them as 'studies' in the sense of being self-educative exercises, and they can be seen as a continuation and expansion of what Eckersberg sought in his own plein air painting trips.[42]

The seemingly random, unpicturesque choice of subject is taken to its extreme in *View from a Window in Toldbodvej Looking towards the Citadel* [25]. The foreground of this small painting is occupied by the strange form of a nearby chimney, beyond which is a

25 · *View from a Window in Toldbodvej Looking towards the Citadel*, c.1833
Statens Museum for Kunst, Copenhagen

26 · *Cigar Seller at the Northern Exit from the Citadel*, 1830
Musée du Louvre, Paris

panoramic view of what Købke could see from the studio he was sharing with Frederik Sødring – it was here that he also painted his portrait of his fellow artist [46]. It must be presumed that this is a work painted directly in front of the motif, looking across the roof-ridge and the prominent chimney, which establish the distance from the studio to the horizon that stretches across the Citadel to the Øresund. Little details establish the Citadel mill, church and the red-roofed military buildings adjacent to the family home. Just visible beyond these are the minuscule crosses of ships' masts. The sky takes up most of the picture surface, and Købke was at this time showing a developed interest in meteorological accuracy. In this respect he was following both Eckersberg, who kept a special diary in which he recorded facts about the weather twice a day until his death, and Johan Christian Dahl. This also echoes as well, perhaps unwittingly, John Constable, whose work of this kind was widely known, but is never specifically cited in any of Købke's letters.[43] In 1803 the English meteorologist Luke Howard had published his definitive scientific classification of clouds in his *Essay on the Modification of Clouds*, using now familiar terminology: nimbus, cirrus, cumulus, stratus, etc., and which prompted Goethe, who had similar interests, to write verse in his praise. At this time, in keeping with other artists, Købke utilised cloud formations as an important part of his compositions, but the scientific findings of meteorology added a further element of realism which was characteristic of the Golden Age outlook. Købke would return with more consistency to this theme in his later works.

Works such as this were not, however, for public consumption, but for the artist's own development, and of the Citadel landscapes only one, as has been mentioned, was exhibited at the annual Charlottenborg exhibition. The fact that *View of the Square in the Citadel Looking towards the Citadel Ramparts* [20] and *View from the Loft of the Grain Store at the Bakery in the Citadel* [22] were exhibited at the Academy, suggests a distinction, namely, that these more precise and finished works, populated by figures, aspired to genre painting. The popularity and legitimacy of genre painting began to thrive during the 1830s as Denmark's post-war fortunes began to prosper and a nationalist revival picked up momentum.

Købke's more sustained engagement with motifs which might be said to carry nationalistic sentiments, was centred around the body of works he produced in the 1830s depicting Frederiksborg Castle. His first foray into this territory, however, came in one of his Citadel paintings, *Cigar Seller at the Northern Exit from the Citadel* [26]. In aspect it is an odd hybrid of a closely observed natural environment and a 'portrait' of a stiffly posed old sailor who has been painted in the studio and not fully integrated with his surroundings. Despite the pretence to 'serious art' born of academic precepts (the Dutch-like still life of objects on the table, the carefully balanced composition of figure and tree, all in finely painted detail) the subject matter – a poor and elderly Danish worker – is unique in Købke's work. The sitter, Jens Fisker, a retired sailor, was a regular feature of Citadel life and sold his goods inside its north gate. He appears again, although unnamed, in the later *Portrait of an Old Sailor* [50]. Købke must have known and talked with his subject on many occasions and he portrays him tenderly and unsentimentally in the possibly symbolic long shadows at the close of the day. Here, presumably without the express intention to proselytise on behalf of the distinct racial or national characteristics of Danish life, Købke nevertheless pre-empted by more than a decade Høyen's exhortations of the mid-1840s for artists to seek out and celebrate ethnic authenticity and the lives of ordinary folk.[44] This would later occasion many paintings of popular life which become a staple of Danish art, but Købke's earlier incursion into this territory is characteristically prompted by a specific and personal fascination with the individuality of his sitter and his environment, of which Købke was himself a part, not merely a spectator.

27 · *View Outside the North Gate of the Citadel*, 1834
Ny Carlsberg Glyptotek, Copenhagen

View Outside the North Gate of the Citadel [27], the same location where Jens Fisker plied his trade, is a work of a different magnitude. This was Købke's first commission from the Fine Arts Society (Kunstforeningen), which brought both prestige and much needed income, and he approached it seriously, both through sketches and, unusually, a study in oils.[45] He laboured on the work intensely and in a letter to his sister Conradine, to whom he appears to have been particularly close, and to whom a number of his surviving letters candidly express his personal feelings, Købke gives us an insight into his state of mind at the time. Most notably, given a tendency throughout his life to oscillate between religious doubts and pious resignation, there is a clear sense of his being in a divine collaboration, from which he draws strength and to which he attributes what success he attains.

> *… it caused me a hard struggle, every day for three whole months I have been struggling with it and sometimes the fight has certainly been very difficult, but then again I have been blessed with lighter moments. – It was certainly about time I pulled myself together as I was almost losing my senses due to the feeling of weakness and ineptitude, but before actually getting started I thought of these words of wisdom: the Lord is strong in the weak and with all my strength I seized God and took the view: it was no concern of mine what he wanted from this when I worked only with the best of intentions and insight … When God gives his creation this feeling you can imagine how happy one is, because one deeply feels an independence of the world and one is sufficient to God and to oneself, in other words when one has God and his justice, one has everything and this feeling of being sufficient to oneself is probably the greatest blessing a painter may have …* [46]

This self-effacing acknowledgement of his limitations was characteristic of Købke's approach. The painter Lorenz Frølich, to whom Købke informally gave artistic instruction (he posed in the painting for the boy in the white trousers), discerned this, noting that 'he shows clearly that everyone can achieve something splendid, something delightful, if only he does not seek to be more than he is.'[47]

Despite such modesty the work is an aesthetic and technical *tour de force* that marks a watershed in the artist's development. From within the North Gate, Købke has chosen an oblique viewpoint that obscures the left side of the bridge, but allows us to look across the moat to the grassy defence systems beyond. The asymmetry of the whole is brilliantly conceived, but the resulting composition artfully conceals this. Instead, this appears to be a simple slice of life preserved as it was at one particular moment, from the exact position of every shadow, to the stacked oars in the dark embrasure on the right, and the casually, though gracefully, posed boys lounging on the bridge. On either side of the view are the blockhouses or *carponiers* that act as a framing device, through which is seen a truncated section of a characteristic red *homeyporte* drawbridge, within the intricacies of which is a daringly realistic detail, the cutting in half of the figure of a woman in a blue dress walking on the bridge. A similar device can be seen in the drawing of Eckersberg on a sketching trip where a tree bisects the horse and cart in the rear [10]. The carefully contrived artifice shows a delight in the 'little sections' or passages that Købke, in a letter two years later, would pinpoint as his strength.[48] This strength is evident here in the intricately detailed grass in the foreground, and the small patches of sunlight dappling the flaking plasterwork on the lower parts of the blockhouses, of which every joint in the brickwork is precisely depicted; even the fore edges of the gatepost tops are stippled with tiny growths of dried moss. It is a world in microcosm, presented rather like a scale model of reality, yet the parts, brilliantly observed as they are, do not distract from the harmony of the whole. In a work that fulfils Eckersberg's insistence on addressing the ideal through the real, the presence of

28 · *The Northern Drawbridge to the Citadel in Copenhagen*, 1837
The National Gallery, London

a divine order is everywhere insinuated. This is also something that finds its counterpart in the intellectual thought of the age. Ørsted's *The Spirit in Nature (Aanden i Naturen)* of 1850, in which he was influenced by the philosopher, Friedrich Schelling, propounded the view that the visible world is a reflection of the divine and that the infinite is present in each moment.[49] Without having the intellectual pretension to such a direct correlation, Købke was clearly not immune to such preoccupations and in this serene image he evokes a scene that posits a structured and benignly governed universe.

The completion of the Citadel pictures marks Købke's leave-taking as in 1833 his father retired and moved with his family to a large, elegant house in Blegdammen just outside the ramparts. Købke returned one last time to this scene in a more romantic rendering, made as a keepsake for his mother in 1837 [28]. But his personal homage to the place that was of crucial importance to him, both in his life and in the development of his artistic practice, is encapsulated in the larger, earlier work. *View Outside the North Gate of the Citadel* has been rightly regarded as Købke's first masterpiece, a painting of truly major significance, a synthesis both of Eckersberg's teaching and beliefs and his own fully developed, independent outlook. It is a coming of age that subsumes and even surpasses the lessons of what he could learn from Eckersberg, and which has subsequently been celebrated as a work that manages to 'elevate the merely observed on to a monumental level … the chosen moment a part of eternity'.[50]

Frederiksborg and National Romanticism ⟚

As Købke said goodbye to his student days and family life in the Citadel he came under fresh influences and began to develop new subjects. In 1832–3 he had completed his studies at Charlottenborg and was sharing a studio with his friend and colleague Frederik Sødring in Toldbodvej, so close to the Citadel that it could be painted from their attic window [25]. This was to be the base from which the two young artists would seek to launch their careers.

Købke remained in contact with Eckersberg and continued to receive personal tuition from him for a few more years. Around this time, however, he also came under the influence of two important figures who contributed significantly to his development as an artist: the sculptor Hermann Ernst Freund [52] and the art historian Høyen. Freund's authority was to be pivotal in Købke's decision, in 1838, to visit Italy, and his influence on the artist is more keenly felt in that part of his career. Høyen's role as mentor to the young painter stemmed from their first recorded meeting in August 1831, at Frederiksborg Castle near the village of Hillerød, some twenty miles north of Copenhagen, a journey Købke occasionally made on foot. It was then not unusual to walk such distances (painters often did likewise on their way to Rome) and he had in any event family connections there. Købke's father had worked as a baker in the village after the British bombardment of his city premises. The artist's visit to Hillerød in July 1831 was in order to nurse his sister Conradine after a difficult childbirth that nearly cost her her life. By this time Købke was on the verge of concluding his academic training and whilst he could have met Høyen at Charlottenborg, where he lectured on Nordic mythology, their meetings at Frederiksborg cemented a more personal relationship and also induced Købke to spend much of the 1830s painting the sixteenth-century Dutch-style castle, the grandest Renaissance palace in Scandinavia. This he did from a variety of viewpoints.

Høyen was to have a powerful influence on the Danish cultural agenda, particularly in shaping a nationalist discourse. In 1856 he would become the first Professor of Art History at the University of Copenhagen, but his views drove the nationalist cause from the late 1820s and even in 1876 his posthumous influence was felt when the last volume of his collected lectures was published, lectures which have had a lasting influence on the development of Danish art history.[51] Høyen's was not a lone voice but, like that of the critic, John Ruskin in Britain, it was heard above others, and he held a similarly intransigent attitude to those who opposed him. Broadly educated and widely travelled, he was influential in the establishment and running of The Fine Arts Society and active in the move to catalogue and preserve the nation's neglected architectural heritage, but his catholic interests extended to all aspects of material culture, local rituals and customs.[52]

Høyen promoted a credo that collective identity stemmed from the land, and found its expression through a nation's art. He urged artists to follow the example of painters such as Friedrich and Dahl in seeking out indigenous and ethnic authenticity, viewed through the prism of human sentiment. By this he intended artists to follow the example of painters who addressed their native lands, but who did so in a manner which resulted not in a dispassionate and factual realism, but which imbued nature with a spiritual ethos. In this respect he advocated Friedrich and Dahl as role models. Friedrich was perhaps the less obvious example to cite since, although his work was well known in Denmark, it was of a more personal nature and imbued with specifically Christian symbolism. Dahl proved to be a more substantial connection between Danish painting and German romanticism, someone who had kept contact with many Danish artists whilst Friedrich pursued a more solitary path. Originally from Norway, which until 1814 had been a part of the Danish kingdom, Dahl was appointed Professor Extraordinary at the Dresden Academy in 1824, but continued to show annually at the Charlottenborg spring exhibitions, which had a strong impact on the generation of young Danish landscape painters after Købke. Johan Thomas Lundbye, P.C. Skovgaard and Dankvart Dreyer, again bolstered by Høyen's influence, most fully aligned their work with an emotive brand of national romantic landscape. In this manner they would seek to fulfil Høyen's insistence that landscape painting should rise above the descriptive, and seek to be a reflection of the human condition, since man's intellectual consciousness of God is manifested in nature.[53]

In a keynote lecture of 1844, 'On the Preconditions for the Development of a Scandinavian National Art', Høyen maintained that contemporary art should 'assert and protect our nationality' just as the Church had used art to promote Christianity:

> *The history of Scandinavia, based on the fundamental characteristics of the country and its people, is the raw material from which the art that we have received fully formed from abroad must be reborn amongst us … Only then will the people recognise in it bones of their bones and flesh of their flesh.*[54]

Joachim Frederik Schouw, Professor of Botany, countered Høyen by arguing that national characteristics were shaped by a nation's history, not its landscapes, arguing that if the latter were so, the Danes would be more German than Scandinavian![55] Schouw's point was well made. Danish and German painters were always close and enjoyed a degree of cultural exchange facilitated by linguistic compatibility (most Danes were familiar with German). The duchies of Schleswig and Holstein, which marked Denmark's southern border with Germany, also provided a place of ethnic blurring since that culture partook of both Danish and German influences. During and after the first conflict over the duchies in 1848–50, relationships with German and German-based painters like Dahl necessarily became more strained and in the post-war period Danish painters of German extraction were 'airbrushed' from the nation's histories of art.[56] But in Købke's time, both at home, and abroad in art centres such as Rome, Danish and German painters enjoyed a friendly reciprocity.

Købke's first visits to Frederiksborg in 1831 coincided with a more forceful promotion by Høyen of a nationalist agenda. At the time of their initial meeting, Høyen was resident at the castle in order to catalogue the royal portrait collection. He and Købke must have quickly recognised that despite the disparity in their intellectual proclivities, and their ages

(Høyen was twelve years his senior), they had shared interests. Høyen had already identified Århus Cathedral in Jutland as a site of major historical significance, and Købke had just returned from there, where he had produced his first detailed architectural painting [31]. Høyen also wrote a paper in the year of their meeting describing Frederiksborg as 'the finest castle in northern Europe.'[57] It seems hardly surprising in these circumstances that Købke was drawn both to Høyen and his advocacy of recording the national heritage in paint.

As a detailed and authentic representation of a monument of national significance, *The Transept of Århus Cathedral* may even have been commenced under Høyen's influence. But by now a craze for the previously disparaged wilderness of Jutland (on the east coast of which Århus lay), once regarded as backward and almost savagely desolate, had gripped the national consciousness, promoted largely by the stories of ordinary folk by Steen Steensen Blicher which were set there.[58] On a later trip to the region Købke produced a simple yet beautiful motif of a well-sweep (a pivoted pole used to raise a bucket), its top brusquely truncated, as is the bulk of the adjacent building [30]. A plain but audaciously composed image of authentic Danish rural life, it seems ready for Blicher's characters to step into it.[59] It may also be indebted to Høyen's promotion of Dutch painting, which acted

30 · *A Well-sweep. On the Right a House*, 1835
Private Collection

31 · *The Transept of Århus Cathedral*, 1830
Statens Museum for Kunst, Copenhagen

32 · Pieter Jansz. Saenredam,
*The Interior of St Bavo's Church, Haarlem
(the 'Grote Kerk')*, 1648
National Gallery of Scotland, Edinburgh

as a foil to the dominance of the neoclassical agenda promoted at the Academy. The simple naturalism of this subject (wholly out of keeping with Friedrich or Dahl), nevertheless addresses aspects of a national identity rooted in the land and its vernacular architecture. At the Academy Høyen now lectured on Dutch painting, where previously he had stressed the traditions of Greece and Rome. In 1836, during the period that Købke was still working at Frederiksborg, Høyen visited The Netherlands and was so impressed by Dutch art (like its Danish counterpart born of middle-class values) that he set about increasing its display within the royal collection.

Despite the vogue for Jutland life, however, Købke's *The Transept of Århus Cathedral* is more rooted in the Dutch tradition than a romantic nationalism, although he has included the genre element of his Århus companions being shown a memorial stone by the local verger. In this, at least, the figures are portrayed taking an interest in the Danish cultural heritage. The older figure is that of the animal painter C.D. Gebauer, whom Købke had met at the home of a student friend, while the younger is Købke's brother Waldemar, a naval cadet, whose vessel was fortuitously offshore at the time. The latter bends down for a closer look, but Gebauer, who was deaf, seems unmoved – perhaps he does not hear the verger's explanation. To the right a farmer and his son look through a screen at the high altar and in the distance an old woman walks with her stick towards the north door. In subject and placing of figures it has some similarities to seventeenth-century Dutch precedents, such as the church interiors of Saenredam [32], emphasising the grandeur and height of the building. But Købke's work is simpler and less majestic, perhaps more concerned with the textures of the decayed and crumbling brick and plasterwork. The white tonality that predominates is everywhere flecked through with colour, from the details of the church furnishings, the yellow Flensburg stone on the floor and the 'discoloured' and peeling walls. Amongst the earliest of Købke's mature works, it shows his characteristic concern for order and structure within a perspective scheme that avoids any easy symmetry.

The lessons learned in the Århus interior in dealing with an architectural subject were continued in the series of paintings, more directly under Høyen's influence, focusing on Frederiksborg Castle. These were executed using a variety of inventive and unconventional perspective schemes and surprising viewpoints. Of their first meeting in August 1831 Høyen noted:

> *A couple of artists are also here: Købke and Marstrand. They are nice young people; especially the first … His is one of those constantly happy natures whose childish and innocent character is immediately captivating and which one esteems because of the seriousness and good fortune with which they work their way forward. A creative genius he hardly has, but a good feeling and tact, a clear head and an easiness when it comes to depiction.*[60]

Købke's reaction was less muted. In his diary for 4 September he writes: 'Spent the evening at Prof. Hoien's [sic]. God! Let me always think like this and give me the strength to carry it out.'[61]

Købke returned to the castle in 1832, after which he was preoccupied with depicting the building throughout the mid-1830s. In two interrelated works, *One of the Small Towers on Frederiksborg Castle* [33] and *Roof Ridge of Frederiksborg Castle with View of Lake, Town and Forest* [34], we see aerial, long-distance vistas of the surrounding landscape supported, as it were, by sections of the roof of the building. Købke's truncated views of this architectural wonder seem wilfully eccentric (he crawled onto the roof to observe the spire), yet they invest these singular parts of the building with a startling presence, their bold and arresting angles of vision making the ordinary seem remarkable. *One of the Small*

33 · *One of the Small Towers on Frederiksborg Castle, c.1834*
The David Collection, Copenhagen

34 · *Roof Ridge of Frederiksborg Castle, with View of Lake, Town and Forest, c.1834–5*
Det danske Kunstindustrimuseet (Danish Museum of Art & Design), Copenhagen

Towers on Frederiksborg Castle in particular partakes strongly of Eckersberg's linear style and has a sense of time arrested (the stork on the chimney top seems unlikely to ever follow its companion into the distant fields) and the atmosphere seems distilled from a soft, diffused light. Købke produced a larger version of this work for the dining room in his parents' house [35]. In *Roof Ridge of Frederiksborg Castle with View of Lake, Town and Forest*, the relationship of foreground to sky is apparently based on the Golden Section (a geometrical ratio favoured by academies to devise compositions with aesthetically pleasing proportions), the painting as a result conveying a more classical harmony. Yet we see little more than the roof-line, the lake and Hillerød beyond, most of the canvas being taken up by an almost featureless sky.[62]

35 · *One of the Small Towers on Frederiksborg Castle*, c.1834–5
Det danske Kunstindustrimuseet (Danish Museum of Art & Design), Copenhagen

Neither painting matches Høyen's dictates that art should record and document national treasures. Yet ironically, whilst these large and ambiguous works, unique in Danish art, were not fully appreciated in their day, they indeed fulfil romantic nationalist ambitions. That the castle could be identified simply from an isolated section spoke eloquently of its significance in national life. The following year Købke completed a very different view of the castle, a work more obviously aligned with the conventional paradigm of romantic nationalism that Høyen favoured. *Frederiksborg Castle in the Evening Light* [37] shows far more conspicuously the sense of immanence that partakes of the Dresden influence of Dahl and Friedrich. It was submitted to a competition in architectural painting organised by the Fine Arts Society at Høyen's suggestion. In the event, the competition was won by Jørgen Roed with a more stringently architectural representation, but the Fine Arts Society nevertheless purchased Købke's work, which may have been perceived to answer the demand that artists venerate their architectural heritage.

Whilst developing various designs for the painting Købke alighted on his chosen view from across the castle lake. Whether he settled on this viewpoint by following precedent or whether he made a deliberate decision is unclear. The motif was popular with artists, and Dahl had painted the view in 1817, which he also executed as an etching and a lithograph. Købke may have been familiar with these.[63] On 12 August 1835, Købke wrote to Jørgen Roed about his progress and included a suitably romantic comment: 'I have just returned from Jægerbagen [*sic*] where I saw lightning around the castle, it looked magnificent!'[64]

His letters reveal this as a testing time and record the tribulations he was encountering with technical and aesthetic challenges. As usual, digestive complaints acted as a barometer of dejection, and his correspondence provides an insight into the personal troubles this caused him. Writing to his sister Conradine he is at pains to justify, on the grounds of health, his refusal to attend a family dinner, but is clearly deeply distressed that this has caused his mother anguish and that the family cannot understand his predicament.[65] Around the same time he told Conradine:

> I am taking my refuge with you tonight, as I know with you I will find a friendly place and I need to do so once in a while to unburden my mind … I have had difficulties lately as my spirit has been under pressure, mainly because of the burden of my work and the bad weather and as is always the case with me my body suffers from this.[66]

He turned, as so often in times of trouble, to reading the Gospels and invoking God's help in performing his tasks to the utmost of his abilities, at which point his mood generally lifted.[67] To Roed on 15 September he confided: 'The castle itself is causing me a lot of trouble, I did want to start all over again'; but he quickly adds: 'Ah! Can you beat it! Hoien [*sic*] is coming this week and is going to stay here for several [days]; my heart is in my

36 · *Frederiksborg Castle.*
View near the Møntbro Bridge, 1836
Statens Museum for Kunst, Copenhagen

mouth when I think of it.'[68] In the event all went well and Købke records spending evenings with Høyen at which they discussed his own work in association with those artists Høyen was studying, including Rembrandt and Claude.[69] He also took time out from painting for family matters, noting: 'Father and Mother have been out here visiting so I have not been painting much … yesterday it was Old Father's birthday, it was a lovely day and I did entertain loving feelings towards my splendid parents.'[70]

Købke did, in fact, commence a second version of the work but time ran out and on the closing date *Frederiksborg Castle in the Evening Light* was submitted. It received some negative criticism for supposed errors in perspective which, the reviewer alleged, destroyed the poetry of the scene.[71] But in a perceptive riposte the philosopher F.C. Sibbern [43], who also wrote poetry and art criticism (and who numbered Kierkegaard amongst his pupils), enthusiastically adumbrated the work's romantic appeal:

37 · *Frederiksborg Castle
in the Evening Light*, 1835
The Hirschsprung Collection,
Copenhagen

*If the other day anyone noticed a man who stood leaning against the wall lost
in contemplation and with his gaze fixed on Mr. Købke's 'Frederiksborg Castle at
Evening' (88) it was the author of these sentences. What was he looking at? A masterpiece; what did he hear? The idyllic tunes of Gessner. What did he feel? The poetry
of the Nordic summer nights.*[72]

In a florid piece of writing Sibbern insisted that 'a true work of art should be poetic'
and commended Købke for evoking the most profound conception of nature, within which
the castle sits as an organic entity. As if to confirm that Købke had here stepped beyond
Eckersberg's example and placed mood and sentiment ahead of his usual realism and clarity,
Sibbern poetically asked: ' … who by a painting such as this is disturbed by an insignificant
incorrectness in perspective would be better off staying with his jars of paint and forget
nature; does one measure nature with a ruler and a compass when pervaded by its infinite
poetry?'[73] The work is not wholly a departure for Købke. The surreal stillness and uniform
mellow light of his rather earlier *One of the Small Towers on Frederiksborg Castle* [35]
are evidence that the heightened mood of the later painting was not alien to his outlook.
The castle reflected in the mirrored surface of the lake, and silhouetted dramatically in dark
crimson against a pale golden, twilight sky, *Frederiksborg Castle in the Evening Light* is
nevertheless singular in Købke's work: a lyrical evocation of a building that was a powerful
totem of national pride and stability. (As if to anticipate the victory of Høyen's heritage-
driven agenda, it would even appear that the first bourgeois tourists have arrived on the
castle lake.)

A small study for an alternative, long-distance view of the castle [38] hints at a closer
association with the German romantic models Høyen was advocating. It makes use of a
moody, more emotional sense of place, and the light that permeates it is executed in sombre
yellow and pink tones, while the elevated viewpoint contributes to the mood of melancholy.
It is a rarity in Danish Golden Age painting for addressing the fluctuation of seasonal
change, something generally eschewed in favour of summer scenery that best lent itself to

38 · *Autumn Landscape, Frederiksborg
Castle in the Middle Distance*, c.1834–5
Ny Carlsberg Glyptotek, Copenhagen

depicting the ideal and unvarying moment. Its place in Købke's work, and its relation to the work of Friedrich and Dahl, will be returned to later, but given that Købke did not proceed further with this study it is hard not to see *Frederiksborg Castle in the Evening Light* as a brilliant but isolated event in his oeuvre. His expressed dissatisfaction with the canvas and its failure to win the competition can hardly have inclined him to carry on in this vein.

Købke was at this time hardly in a resolute state of mind. His letters show him preoccupied with personal matters that must have been to the otherwise earnest young artist a pleasant distraction from such weighty issues. In October 1836, the year he completed his last major work on the Frederiksborg theme, his letters show him enjoying an excursion to the castle with his fiancée Sanne, with whom he says he is planning to study German (no hint here of any preparations to visit Italy!) and on whose portrait he announces his commencement.[74] The young couple were to be married on 7 November the following year.

It seems plain that as his final Frederiksborg canvas was nearing completion, Købke had other, happier considerations than Høyen's nationalist stratagems in mind. His state of irresolution is reflected in the fact that *Frederiksborg Castle. View near the Møntbro Bridge* [36], depicting only a section of the building, was started even as his competition piece was drying. It suggests that Købke had been consistently failing to find a satisfactory conception. This painting is much tighter in its style and returns to the artist's characteristic use of an asymmetrical viewpoint. It is not, however, merely a piece of faithfully documented architectural reportage: Købke removed a small promontory within the lake and rearranged the foreground foliage to give a clearer view (through the arches of the bridge) of how the castle sits in the water. And true to Høyen's belief in period authenticity, he 'edited' out an eighteenth-century stair turret.[75] The work suggests a return to Eckersberg's sense of clarity and precision in terms of line and meticulously rendered detail. But the oblique view, the translucent, pale blue of the sky, the subdued greens of the trees and foliage, and the varied pinks of the brickwork hint at a debt to the German romantic influence that Købke must surely have heeded at Høyen's insistence.

These matters aside, there is nothing in Købke's letters, beyond a mild patriotism and ingrained respect for authority, to suggest a political animal of any sort. In a letter to Roed he noted: 'I do not do much when it comes to reading and I do not attach great importance to it, I consider it something not part of our matter as we probably must read or rather see nature differently from the poet.'[76] Put plainly, his devotion was to the visual, and, most consistently, to the glory of the Almighty. Yet Købke is now regarded as epitomising a distinctively Danish vision, and it would be true to say that occasionally his personal outlook aligned sufficiently with the beliefs of those of a more polemical persuasion to allow him to produce paintings that have subsequently become fixed in the national consciousness. The Frederiksborg works were a sustained engagement in the field of nationalist subject matter, an experiment bolstered no doubt by Høyen, and if the artist did not ultimately wish to become a spokesman for such concerns, his work of this kind shows a marked receptiveness towards the stimulus of these ideas. Elsewhere, expressions of national esteem would find eloquent outlet in his oeuvre, but Købke would undoubtedly have agreed with his friend, the artist Wilhelm Marstrand, when he declared:

> *What have politics, nationality and taxes to do with painterly effects and beautiful lines? What does national art mean? Does it mean politically Danish from border to border and all things within those boundaries? Or does it mean Nordic, including Nordic history and the Sagas? ... No, just as the same sun shines over the entire world, art has no boundaries; it serves only beauty and truth.*[77]

Portraiture

Throughout his career, and to the end of his life, Købke painted a large body of portraits which are best regarded as a separate entity. Although still deemed low in the artistic hierarchy, portraiture at this time offered artists the most secure prospect of professional viability, and since commissions for other kinds of work were few and far between, artists could not afford to ignore this potential source of income. The nature of portraiture did, however, mutate during the course of the Golden Age. As the effects of absolutism were eroded through the decades up to its abolition in 1849, and with the institution of a parliamentary constitution, the emerging bourgeoisie increasingly sought images that would confirm their new position and values within society. The patronage of court and nobility gave way to that of civil servants and businessmen, and artists responded with intimate, often idyllic, images, but marked by a degree of psychological candour. Large family groups [40] illustrated the virtues and stability of middle-class domesticity, where every nuance of dress and furniture expressed a cultivated prosperity, or encoded rank and duty. Frequently such works would include depictions of earlier family portraits, in order to emphasise a sense of lineage and dependability.[78]

Købke followed suit in terms of the age's need for detailed realism and compositional clarity, but was also drawn to the probing of personality. With one exception, his portraits are of single figures, frequently placed close to the front of the painting in a way that allows for a seemingly direct and personal encounter with the sitter. It is no doubt this proclivity of Købke's to scrutinise personality rather than social status that might in part explain his lack of major public portrait commissions. To a large extent, therefore, Købke has left us an intimate gallery of family and friends that generated little remuneration – we have no confirmation that he was paid for such works. In one instance, when his sister Sophie wished to order a portrait of her father-in-law Major J.J. Krohn (seen giving the orders in *View of the Square in the Citadel Looking towards the Citadel Ramparts* [20]), she offered payment of a ring set with an antique stone.[79] The largesse of acquaintances may have helped occasionally but in many instances, such as portraits exchanged with fellow artists, works took the form of gifts.

Whilst Bendz viewed the portrait treadmill as 'something approaching death',[80] Købke embraced a potential career in this jobbing activity, establishing himself in 1832 in a

studio apartment he shared with Sødring, with the prospect of setting up business. Quite why the world didn't beat a path to his door is a mystery as he rapidly evolved a deft and brilliant ability not merely to capture likeness, but to reveal convincingly the inner disposition of his sitters, in which his personal intimacy with them proved a vital factor.

Købke painted only one self-portrait [1], a frank and ingenuous piece of self-analysis, engaging in its earnest sincerity. With perhaps just a hint of a romantically rebellious hairstyle, the effect is otherwise of a solid and dependable young burgher. Nor has Købke sought to play down his boyish, ruddy complexion (he was then just twenty-three years old) that so captivated the Italian women on his later travels that they would pinch their cheeks in imitation of his. As with many of his portraits, Købke has concentrated solely on his own image and included no hint of a setting, leaving the viewer no option but to engage with his youthful countenance.

This work was painted in Købke's studio. His close neighbours in the same building were Høyen and his wife, Birgitte Westengaard, and he produced a charming and elaborately costumed likeness of her the same year [41]. It was probably painted to celebrate the couple's marriage in 1832, when the thirty-five-year-old Birgitte finally concluded their fourteen-year engagement! Mrs Høyen was a caring and protective friend to Købke, and he depicts her sympathetically and with great affection. The simple frontal pose against a completely plain background, the frank engagement with character, the meticulous description of textures, the warm colour range set against the cool whites of the headdress, all show an early and astonishing accomplishment. Indeed, with the exception of the penetrating portraits of Christian Albrecht Jensen, Købke had no equal as a portrait painter. Eckersberg, although peerless in fixing an exact likeness, seldom probed deeply into character, and his sitters often appear as little more than superficial imitations. Jensen's model of freely handled paint, combined with deep psychological insight (he was frequently likened to Hals), was more in keeping with Købke's approach and he can be seen consistently aligning himself with this manner.

Købke's sensitivity in the scrutiny of character was always present, regardless of age, gender or social standing. His portrait of Høyen's mother, for example [42], is a

40 · Wilhelm Marstrand,
The Waagepetersen Family, 1836
Statens Museum for Kunst, Copenhagen

41 · *Portrait of Mrs B. Høyen,*
née Westengaard, 1833
The Hirschsprung Collection, Copenhagen

42 · *Portrait of Inger Margrethe Høyen,*
née Schrøder. The Art Historian
N.L. Høyen's Mother, 1832
Statens Museum for Kunst, Copenhagen

profoundly sympathetic – even beautiful – characterisation of an elderly woman, which at the same time delights in the endless variety of her face and costume. A self-made woman of plain habits and unspoiled character, Mrs Høyen was the daughter of a Jutland gardener and later married a distiller who worked his way up to own his own distillery. Høyen credited her with awakening his interest in art. She led a simple, contented existence, often taking her meals with the employees and was by all accounts a mild, wise and imaginative individual.[81] Købke clearly senses these traits and seems to map her life as it is inscribed in the contours of her kindly and unpretentious face, radiant against the dark background.

A similarly incisive depiction of character in an elderly sitter is a portrait drawing of the philosopher F.C. Sibbern [43], which was commissioned by his university students, a subject with whom the artist became good friends. Sibbern, like Ørsted, was a notable product of Golden Age intellectual diversity, a true polymath, remembered now as an exponent of natural philosophy and a pioneer of modern psychology. He also wrote novels and poetry and turned his hand to journalism – which included his positive review and spirited defence of Købke's *Frederiksborg Castle in the Evening Light*. In an awe-inspiring technical *tour de force*, Købke captures a gentleness and humanity which is offset by the piercing gaze of this redoubtable intellectual, who confronts us in what appears to be characteristically composed body language.

When working with child sitters, where character was undeveloped, Købke also showed great intuition. His tiny portrait of Ida Thiele, the eighteen-month-old daughter of the art historian, Just Mathias Thiele, secretary of the Academy, is an extraordinary example [45]. One of Købke's rare commissions, it was intended as a birthday present for her grandfather. In seeking to keep the young Ida (who inspired Hans Christian Andersen's

43 · *Portrait of Frederik Christian Sibbern*, 1833
Department of Prints and Drawings, Statens Museum for Kunst, Copenhagen

44 · Wilhelm Bendz, *A Young Artist (Ditlev Blunck) Looking at a Sketch in a Mirror*, 1826
Statens Museum for Kunst, Copenhagen

story 'Little Ida's Flowers') from fidgeting, Købke alighted on the stratagem of having her draw with chalks. The result shows her absorbed in her creative activity, a convincingly alert and sentient individual, rather than one of the stereotypical, doll-like images of children. The completed work was presented to her grandfather by Ida, who, dressed as a country maid, carried it to him secured to her back. Clearly a precocious child she appeared to grasp her role in the surprise and duly turned to present her painted image at the appropriate moment.[82] For Købke a commission from so important a figure as Thiele was an honour, but it did not inhibit his desire to experiment. The inventive composition and handling of large, bright colour masses against a near neutral background display bold aesthetic ingenuity.

Despite the general paucity of commissions, Købke was always busy. In 1833, for example, there are works dated to almost every month of the year.[83] Nowhere are his prodigious talents more evident at this time than in the portrait of his friend and studio colleague, the landscape painter Frederik Sødring [46]. It is important to remember when confronted with paintings of such complexity and accomplishment that this is the work of someone in their early twenties. On the day he presented it to Sødring as a birthday present, Købke was only five days into his twenty-third year. Yet everything about this small canvas exudes maturity, both its ambition and its immaculately structured realisation. At the same time its sophisticated content is balanced by the simplicity and sincerity of the way in which the sitter's presence is achieved.

Købke invites us through a collection of motifs to consider the enclosed space of the studio as a slightly dishevelled, partly domestic world where art is 'produced'. Part of that singular world – an easel, a picture frame – are reflected in the oval mirror hung haphazardly across the centre of the door. The world beyond, however, is inferred by the closed doors, seemingly blocked by the small table as well, but with a prominent latch behind Sødring's head. The panels of the doors are also awash with the white light of contemporary Copenhagen, entering from a window, presumably a high one, on the right, which casts a series of overlapping shadows throughout the lower section of the painting. A print of a cow (perhaps after Paulus Potter)[84] and others of Roman ruins pinned to the door, are generally assumed to be more straightforwardly symbolic, representing the two main Golden Age precepts – working from nature, and striving for the ideal. These beliefs are what had so far informed Sødring's development, but the emphasis is now seen to be turning towards the plein air practices marked by the portable artist's stool stowed in the corner.

Further and deeper investigation of all or any of these apparent associations would doubtless be fruitful, and have been taken up in the past to illuminate the many directions of speculative thought the portrait might be felt to encapsulate: the clash of artistic impulses, the juxtaposition of history and contemporaneity, the role and ambition of artists in modern bourgeois Denmark, the function of art as a mirror on reality, and, perhaps more credibly, the symbolic associations between the ivy and friendship.

If Købke was thinking in this way, he would not have been unique, and it may be that he was following the example of Wilhelm Bendz, who, from 1826, painted several pictures of artists at work which were infused with a detailed symbolism.[85] Bendz's work, however, is indicative of a more self-conscious tendency of artists, to depict themselves in a manner that enhances their standing as creative individuals. In an essentially romantic image, Bendz paints his colleague Ditlev Blunck at work on a portrait of another artist, the battle painter Jørgen Sonne [44]. The overt and dense symbolism of the work alludes to (amongst many things) ideas such as the permanence of art over the transience of life (represented traditionally by the skull) or of the creative spirit that art can set free (the caged bird top right).

But this detailed and rather literal symbolism, adopted from Dutch precedents, is more or less absent from Købke's portrait which, far from presenting Sødring as some kind of intellectual, instead concentrates on a range of purely visual descriptive delights: the youthful, pink-cheeked artist inelegantly slouched but self-composed, palette knife in hand ready to begin work; the meticulously painted still life on the mahogany table (possibly including some sketchbooks) selected for its range of textures and subtle colour harmonies; the brilliant red box which draws the eye to the only point of pure colour in an otherwise faultless ensemble of cool tones. The abrupt cropping of all four sides of the composition is particularly daring, and few passages in Købke's art can compare to the astonishing detail of Sødring's brocaded silk waistcoat, striped shirt and black velvet collar. Touchingly inscribed on its reverse, 'Presented to me by my friend! Ch: Købke on my birthday 31 May 1832', the carefully organised composition might be considered as simply a means to create an unrivalled image of intimacy, relaxation and spontaneity, where the mirror might, after all, be just a mirror, and not a neo-Platonic symbol of life's illusion.[86]

This would not, however, discount the brilliantly realised detail, of which the whole is necessarily a product. In one of his few direct comments on artistic theory, Købke told Jørgen Roed:

46 · *Portrait of the Landscape Painter Frederik Sødring*, 1832
The Hirschsprung Collection, Copenhagen

I have been seriously thinking about what it is a painter should and can present by
his means, and I come more and more to feel that we can only express ourselves,
or at least I, in little sections assuming that I start out from the total impression of
the painting, which we both agree is the right thing, only it all depends on the little
sections being in the right place. I have also arrived at much more clarity on this
point through several discussions I have had with Freund and in which indeed I have
really felt consolation and encouragement.[87]

Købke suggests that having taken the total impression as his point of departure, his
art finds fulfilment in the close attention to detail. This approach can be demonstrated in

many of his portraits, for example, *Portrait of the Naval Lieutenant D. Christen Schifter Feilberg* [47].

The sitter, aged twenty-seven, was well known to Købke, a brother and sister of the artist having married into the Feilberg family. He was, by all accounts, a strikingly handsome and self-assured, if arrogant, individual from whom Købke endured a degree of sarcastic condescension. (His nemesis came in 1851 when he was brought home from London in a state of insanity and died shortly afterwards.) This alliance of confidence and conceit is beautifully summarised in this elegant cocktail of rank and character as the young naval officer pulls on his glove and engages Købke, and, of course, the viewer with nonchalant indifference. Its effectiveness rests on such 'little sections' as the red and gold touches that animate the surface, the irregular black outline of the left sleeve, the hat against the cool

48 · *Portrait of the Animal Painter Christian Holm*, 1834
Statens Museum for Kunst, Copenhagen

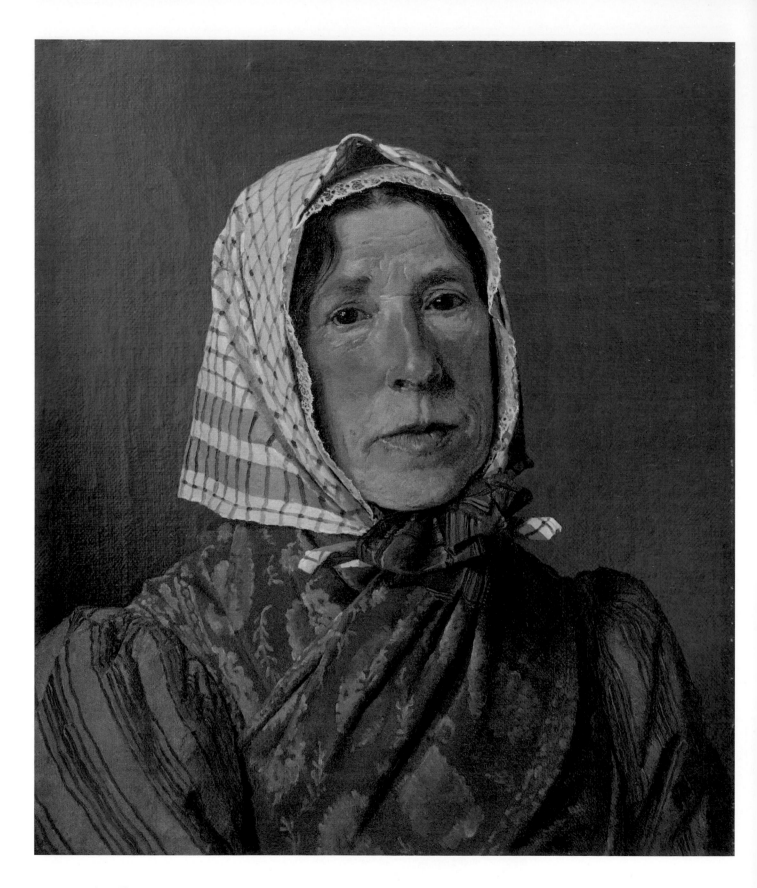

49 · *Portrait of an Old Peasant Woman,* 1832
Randers Kunstmuseum, Randers

50 · *Portrait of an Old Sailor*, 1832
Statens Museum for Kunst, Copenhagen

blue background, and the dangling fingers of the empty glove that appear below the red cuff. Such details, or 'sections' are held together with an ease that conceals the self-conscious effort that has gone into a quite sensual image, one that even has an air of Renaissance *sprezzatura* – a graceful, although contrived, sense of ease. Sibbern noted this ability to make the parts coalesce, saying of Købke's art that though it was expressive 'even in all the smaller sections' it was ultimately 'an unity, technically as well as ideally'.[88]

Købke's ability as a portraitist was also combined with an interest in what might be termed progressive subject matter. The nationalistic preoccupation with ethnic authenticity, bolstered by literary forays such as Blicher's stories, saw the rise of a type of genre painting that described the lives and customs of ordinary Danes. In a process that has been called a 'cultural decentralisation', this shifted the focus from cosmopolitan Copenhagen to the so-called lower orders and the rural hinterland.[89] But where artists had tended to locate the working class within scenes of rustic simplicity, or engaged with such subjects through a use of humour, Købke produced two portraits which took a different view. Both portraits are of anonymous sitters and speak as much of conditions of age and class and of how their countenances have been marked by their lives, as of their individuality. Simply titled, *Portrait of an Old Peasant Woman* and *Portrait of an Old Sailor* [49, 50], Købke has approached them with a degree of fidelity and realism that both maps their outward appearance and reveals an inner identity, despite their remaining nameless. The paintings are grave, dignified masterpieces that profoundly engage the viewer with their strong sense of presence, something that compensates for their anonymity. Each individual is unique, powerful and compelling, yet Købke's intensive painterly labour has been expended on works that were surely not commissioned and which were unlikely to find a buyer.

During the mid-1830s Købke made a number of more ambitious and monumental portraits, but he was always at ease working in a wide range of dimensions. His *Portrait of the Painter Wilhelm Marstrand* of 1836 [39] shows him still working on a small scale, eliminating setting so as to concentrate on his fellow artist's carefree personality. Marstrand, who was amongst the foremost painters of the day, specialised in anecdotal and humorous themes. A man of overwrought temperament, he was known to his friends as 'the Berserker'. In a work intended for Marstrand's mother, Købke substitutes Marstrand's habitual pipe (of which she disapproved) with a tiny rose, hinting also at a cavalier attitude. The portrait depicts a highly informal personality with a degree of light-heartedness, even irreverence, that is elsewhere absent in Købke's art. By contrast the elegant, harmonious *Portrait of the Animal Painter Christian Holm* [48] has a more serious quality, though still executed on a tiny canvas (slightly smaller than a sheet of A4 paper). The sitter rests his folded arms, almost insolently, on the back of a chair, while the whole figure is pushed slightly to the left, leaving a strip of background visible on the right, running from top to bottom of the picture space. This hints at a setting, but no details are shown. Hot tempered and contrary by nature, Holm was a pupil of Gebauer (the elderly figure in Købke's painting of Århus Cathedral). He avoided Eckersberg's circle and preferred to study in Munich. A close friend of Sødring's, this portrait was painted as a farewell gift before he left for Germany. Even in such a small work, Købke has captured the essence of the self-confident and strong-willed painter.

As he began more frequently to work on a much larger scale, Købke made few, if any, concessions in terms of integrity and candidness, but the more monumental works lent themselves less well to intimacy with his subject. His sensitive, but unidealised portrait of his cousin, and then fiancée, Sanne (they were married in 1837), for instance, shows a more polished and austere approach, as if standing further back to take in much of the figure as well as the face – a strategy that has resulted in a more detached portrait [51]. It was perhaps natural that Købke should experiment with works of novel dimensions initially through portrayals of those closest to him, and this is one of several similar images of family and friends produced at this time. More limited in their colour schemes, these works appear crisper and subject to greater restraint in their careful poses and sharp definition.

This approach permeates the still larger and more ambitious *Portrait of the Sculptor Hermann Ernst Freund* [52], who, after Eckersberg, and along with Høyen, became the closest and most important mentor to Købke. Freund, characterised as a morose and embittered man who lived in the shadow of Thorvaldsen, is sometimes credited with being a baleful influence on the young artist. It is asserted that Freund imparted his dark mood of despondency, 'almost resulting in a change of personality' to the pietistic Købke.[90] It is clear, however, that Købke, though in awe of Freund, admired him and found in him an intellectual and artistic guide. He acknowledged Freund's 'consolation and encouragement', and told Constantin Hansen and Jørgen Roed in Rome: 'I have learned a lot from him and

have got completely different concepts on art since you left us.'[91] On Freund's death, Købke's letters express his profound and sincere mourning, summed up laconically as 'Freund is missed everywhere.'[92] It was also largely due to Freund's enthusiasm for the antique (along with the cajoling of Købke's brother-in-law, F.C. Krohn) that the reluctant artist was all but pushed out of the sculptor's door with orders to visit Italy. Freund, whose depression was borne mainly of a conviction that the achievements of the classical world were beyond improvement, a belief that seems to have sapped his vitality, appears, however, to have been considerate and generous in seeking to further Købke's career.

Since Thorvaldsen (to whom Freund was an assistant in Rome) had effectively cornered the market in neoclassical commissions, it fell to the Bremen-born Freund to seek instead to integrate the Nordic Pantheon into the artistic repertoire, as signified by the sculptor's own statue of the Norse god Odin seen in the foreground of Købke's portrait. But Freund was also fascinated by the classical legacy. When, in 1828, he returned reluctantly (on the king's instructions) to Copenhagen, after nearly eleven years in Italy, he took up a professorship at the Royal Danish Academy the following year, and set about decorating his academic apartments in the Pompeian style. The ornamentation of his home, which is still largely intact, received huge attention at the time.[93] It is here that Købke portrays him, and again, despite the imposing scale of this canvas and the eminence of the sitter, we are confronted with a portrait of an intimate friend and mentor. Freund wears a smock embroidered with classical borders, seated on a Greek chair of his own design in his Pompeian room. Yet his thoughts are on Nordic mythology as he regards the statue of Odin. This was a later addition, as can be seen from the curious effects caused by the under-painting now showing through the top layer of paint, so that the statue appears to be materialising (or is it disappearing?) under the sculptor's gaze.

With hindsight many commentators have regarded this work, left incomplete on Freund's death, as the image of a remote and resentful man isolated in his neoclassical Xanadu. That Freund fails to make eye contact with the viewer speaks of a certain inaccessibility of character, yet there is good reason to understand this as the intellectual contemplation of a man absorbed by the creative act. If it lacks the warmth and charm of other portraits, it is in keeping with the serious nature of Freund's profession. A majestic work in Købke's oeuvre, it is ripe for reassessment, as indeed is Freund himself.[94]

Købke painted portraits throughout his life, even during his travels through Italy, where commissions augmented his meagre allowance. His best portraits belong to his mature period during the 1830s, but the twilight of his career also yields examples of great quality. His output constitutes a major achievement of Golden Age art and culture: images of candid warmth and psychological penetration, delighting in naturalistic detail and life's 'little sections' yet never losing sight of the humanity of his sitters. Købke's letters show that this was not arrived at easily, no matter how graceful and effortless the results might seem. On finishing a portrait of his sister Cecilie he wrote:

> … it is such a strange feeling completing a work, I never know whether to laugh or to cry. – When I think of all the bitter hours the work has caused me and the troubles I have had, and also the multitude of sins which are not part of my intention or my conviction, I do get sad, yet when I think of what I have overcome I feel so light at heart.[95]

Sødring's portrait can be seen as the supreme exemplar of this dedication. Its unconventional structure and its freshness have only increased its appeal over nearly two centuries. Its complexity, and yet simple integrity, are powerful testimony to the dedication, insight and sensitivity that Købke brought to a genre to which he made a unique contribution.

52 · *Portrait of the Sculptor Hermann Ernst Freund*, c.1838
The Royal Danish Academy of Fine Arts, Copenhagen

Blegdammen ⪦

53 · Detail from *View from
Dosseringen near the Sortedam
Lake Looking towards Nørrebro*,
c.1838 [58]
Statens Museum for Kunst,
Copenhagen

In October 1833, the year Købke painted his only self-portrait, and shortly before he received his first commission from the Fine Arts Society (Kunstforeningen) for *View Outside the North Gate of the Citadel* [27], the extended Købke family exchanged their home in the Citadel for grander premises in the rural outskirts of the city at Blegdammen, which took its name from the traditional site of the bleaching grounds. In an age when several extended families might huddle in a single tenement, this substantial house, comprising twenty-three rooms, must have seemed luxurious. The 1840 census shows sixteen people living here (three of whom were servants), including one of Købke's unmarried sisters, several of the adult sons, and Købke and his family.[96] It is not known precisely when Købke moved in. The first surviving letter from Blegdammen dates from October 1834, and by the autumn of 1835 he had set up his studio here.[97] From the 1845 census it would appear that the house was subdivided, with a separate apartment for Købke, Sanne, and their four-year-old son Peter. The apartment was on the extreme right of the building, recorded in a later photograph [54]. Life at the house was hospitable, convivial, hectic and, one might imagine, rather noisy, as, at various times, Købke's parents provided lodgings for their numerous offspring. In a humorous letter from Rome imagining a typical day at Blegdammen, Købke's brother-in-law F.C. Krohn gives a spirited account of the family members, old and young, warmly vying with, and baiting, each other in friendly exchange and competition. Above the din, he speculates, can be discerned Mathiis (Købke's family nickname) kissing Sanne so loudly 'that it can be heard throughout the room' whilst she 'sits quite silent in contemplation of her hero at work'.[98]

The house also had a large garden that bordered Lake Sortedam to the rear, where Købke was to paint some of his finest works and studies. Whilst he continued during the 1830s with various projects, notably the visits to Frederiksborg and his growing portfolio of portraits, the works done around Blegdammen and adjacent Dosseringen (the embankment) can be regarded as a discrete and important phase in his art. Here too he revealed his first sustained interest in decorative art, which he later seriously considered as a career. He decorated the family dining room with the two large scenes from Frederiksborg [34, 35] which were hung balancing trompe l'œil paintings of Thorvaldsen's *Day* and *Night* each set in their own panelling [55].[99] As a contrapuntal pairing they comprise an interesting aesthetic – the Frederiksborg paintings contemporary, unconventional, the tondos complete, composed and traditional. It was an arrangement that suggests an innovative feeling for decorative possibilities. It is sometimes assumed that Købke assisted in decorating Freund's apartment, and it is certainly known that he helped Heinrich Eddelien, a fellow pupil of Eckersberg's, when, in late 1836, he was having difficulties meeting his deadline to complete a series of Pompeian decorations for Prince Christian Frederik (who would become King Christian VIII in 1839) at the Amalienborg Palace.[100] However, it was not until his return from Italy in 1840 that Købke would take up decorative art in earnest.

His first major work at Blegdammen, *View of a Street in Østerbro, outside Copenhagen* [57], was his most ambitious to date, not merely in size, but in its attempt to define the specificity of a particular time and place. The scene is close to the family's new home, and is the location also of 'Petersborg', where Købke's grandfather established the bakery that British forces had annihilated in 1807. It had, therefore, a personal significance, but Købke also sensed in it a strong Arcadian flavour illustrating the proximity and interdependency of town and country. The fisherwomen rest as they walk their produce to the city market, whilst country folk in their 'Sunday best' come in by cart. Cows head out of town to graze on nearby Blegdammen Common (where Købke mentions sketching these animals, something new in his art)[101] whilst various Copenhagen citizens promenade in the shade of the suburban mansions, which are faithfully recorded.[102] The imposing house in the centre is 'Rosendal', now long gone but still commemorated by its location noted over the lintel of the building that has taken its place. The building to its right, entered by the high archway, was an adjunct of the University of Copenhagen where F.C. Sibbern and other cultural luminaries met for intellectual gatherings. Sibbern family tradition maintains that it is the top-hatted philosopher and his wife who can be seen approaching it beneath the trees.

To facilitate his work Købke utilised the perspective-octant devised by Eckersberg. With the help of this instrument he executed a greater than usual number of studies, done in situ, from which he produced highly detailed drawings that were then transferred to the canvas, but incorporating subtle changes where necessary. Two drawings of 1836, for example, show that he removed a modern street light, erected in 1830, presumably for aesthetic reasons.[103] The work was completed in October 1836 and on the fifteenth day of that month he noted the approval of Eckersberg and Freund, adding that he felt its strength resided in its restraint.[104]

It was exhibited at the Fine Arts Society with other sketches and paintings in January 1837 and was reviewed as being the most outstanding work yet from a painter 'who now

54 · Unknown photographer, *Master Baker Købke's House on Blegdammen seen from the Garden*, c.1890
Photography Collection, The Royal Library, Copenhagen

55 · *Day and Night*, c.1834–5
The David Collection, Copenhagen

56 · *View from the Limekiln with*
Copenhagen in the Background, 1836
Nivaagaards Malerisamling / Nivaagaard
Picture Gallery Collection, Nivå

ranks among the best'. The review concluded: 'This piece clearly shows us how a masterly perception and an excellent execution can create a beautiful and interesting work from the most common subject.'[105] Købke had not always been free from criticism concerning the triviality of his subjects, which here is turned to a triumph. The serenity of the scene, with its Vermeer-like stillness and clarity of light, transfixes the viewer. It is tempting to speculate that the writer Jens Peter Jacobsen had this scene in mind when, in his 1880 novel *Niels Lyhne*, he has one of his characters romantically reminisce:

> ... *the strange Copenhagen she discovered when she came in from the country one morning. It seemed so fantastic in its bustle and sunshine, with its whitewashed window frames and the smell of fruit in the streets; the buildings looked unreal in the bright light, and it was as if a silence lay over them which the noise and rumbling of wagons could not disturb* [106]

Despite the beguiling simplicity of the scene it is, of course, to an extent contrived – insignificant or accidental details are omitted in preference for the picturesque – but Købke convinces us of the subject's reality. Sharply observed, painted from nature, and packed with refined details or 'little sections' (it is possible to glimpse into the windows of several buildings), the painting shows more than the artist could see at a particular moment, but all that he has observed over a period of time. In this the canvas strikes a transcendental key, where time is arrested, or suggests an eternity, evoking the ideal within the real. It is Schelling's notion of an infinity glimpsed within the ordinary. That religious connotation might seem also contained in the vast sky which dwarfs the human activity.[107] A similar note of the transcendental, where the heavens preside over the markers of human activity,

57 · *View of a Street in Østerbro outside Copenhagen. On the Right 'Rosendal', in the Background 'Petersborg'*, 1836
Statens Museum for Kunst, Copenhagen

seems implicit in a small work of the same year, *View from the Limekiln with Copenhagen in the Background* [56], in which Købke has also made use of his studies of cows. Both the livestock and the simple architecture are carefully structured after seventeenth-century Dutch precedents, in which this tendency to utilise the motif of the humble cottage in tandem with local landscape, realistically observed, became a characteristic of Netherlandish painting.[108] Here Købke adapts that tradition to nineteenth-century Denmark.

Yet the painting has the feel of something unpremeditated, and has similarities to the Østerbro street scene with its matter-of-factness, low horizon, luminously vaulted sky and bright sunlight. The setting is the northern outskirts of Copenhagen near the Citadel, the busy Øresund visible on the left, the naval harbour at Nyholm far right, and miniscule figures strolling by the shore. The little yellow cottage is that of a 'strandrider', a calling between customs official and salvage officer who had charge of a specific section of coast.[109] The family may have supplemented their income from the sale of milk to the city, as was common for civil servants with sufficient ground to graze cattle.

The paradox inherent in works such as this is their 'syncretic' approach to art – that is, the attempted union of seemingly opposing principles. Most of the best Golden Age paintings wrestle with the apparent contradiction in presenting a highly detailed, naturalistic realism, allied to a conceptual idealism. Even in its most descriptive form, art still sought to address the underlying ideal that insisted the observable world was shaped by deity. The picturesque idealism in Købke's unassuming work, and others like it, is not, therefore, a form of escapism or a rose-tinted denial of life's less attractive aspects. Rather, it is the conscious desire to cast nature in its most noble light, which in turn is a surrogate for the divine authorship that a devout mind like Købke ascribed to the visible world.[110] These beliefs find their summation in *View from Dosseringen near the Sortedam Lake Looking towards Nørrebro* [58]. In an image which seems emblematic of Denmark with its pristine serenity and modest beauty, it became, perhaps, an elegy for the artist. In 1838 he left for Italy before it was exhibited at Charlottenborg and on his return two years later he produced no more finished works on Danish subjects.

The view is set on the edge of the man-made lake at the bottom of Købke's garden, an adjunct of the city's water-supply system. Although the stretch of water was artificial, its treatment is gently romanticised and filtrated through the mildest of nationalistic sentiments – a static, poetic, yet monumental evocation of a late summer's afternoon, its cool tones warmed by the violet glow on the water. A low-key, underplayed narrative (leave-taking or arrival), is woven into a work admirable in the restraint Købke rightly identified as his strength. We see no faces, read no emotion, barely sense the body language of the participants, but the simplest things are rendered beautiful: the soft, radiant light, falling on the women's clothing (with the stillness of Vermeer), the fragile shape of the little jetty and the humble vegetation on the banks, painted with botanical accuracy. Its companion piece, *View from Dosseringen near the Sortedam Lake Looking towards Østerbro* [59], is equally breathtaking. The scene, the same stretch of water but viewed in the opposite direction, has a similar balance and sense of quiet spaciousness, though the narrative, such as it is, is more pronounced. The painting was well reviewed, but with a caveat:

> In almost all his latest work this artist has distinguished himself by conscientious truth and simplicity, but unfortunately also by a conspicuous indifference to his choice of subjects; the latter is highly regrettable as nature possesses much that is dull and ignoble which cannot serve as a worthy object for art.[111]

This denigration of the 'dull and ignoble' in nature may have been aimed at the mass of scrub and weeds that occupy the right foreground in *View from Dosseringen near the*

58 · *View from Dosseringen near the Sortedam Lake Looking towards Nørrebro*, c.1838
Statens Museum for Kunst, Copenhagen

Sortedam Lake Looking towards Nørrebro, and which would ordinarily have been omitted from ideal landscapes. However, Købke had already been making for his own pleasure a series of little paintings of undergrowth, trees and water at nearby Dosseringen [63]. Some might be tempted to call this subject matter insignificant, but, in fact, for Købke they were a means of finding the underlying grammar in nature, on which the larger structures would be built.

Affirmation of the painting's values came when King Christian VIII purchased *View from Dosseringen near the Sortedam Lake Looking towards Nørrebro* for the royal collection, the first of only two such instances in Købke's career. Two years later, however, it was removed to his private apartments. Whether the king was unable to live without it, or whether he sought to obscure it from public view, has generated some speculation, which focuses on the motif of the Danish flag. Its inclusion must be regarded as a deliberate stratagem, since it does not appear in the preliminary studies. Essentially a symbol of royalty as well as nationhood, unauthorised flying of the 'Dannebrog' was banned on 7 January 1834 and not repealed until 1854. Why then does Købke, here, and in the pendant piece, introduce this prohibited emblem?[112] No other work between the dates of the ban appears to do so except in an historical and patriotic context.

59 · *View from Dosseringen near the Sortedam Lake Looking towards Østerbro*, 1838
Museum Oskar Reinhart am Stadtgarten, Winterthur

It has been surmised that the ban sought to prevent the flag being misused as a symbol of the growing nationalism of the 1830s, which thus might make Købke's use of it some kind of indicator of national pride, but it is impossible to be certain. The ban, by Frederik VI, appears to have been connected with the needs of diplomacy. In 1832 he rejected requests by various foreign consuls to fly their flags, considering this to be somehow a hazard to the nation. But rather than muddy international relations he balanced the situation by also banning unauthorised flying of the Danish flag.[113]

There are no records of any citizen being prosecuted for infringing the ban, and possibly it was rarely respected. The flag's prominent appearance in Købke's painting, however, must be seen as purposeful, a sign perhaps that art cannot be tied by temporal legislation or ideology. Another suggestion has been that Købke indicates the inexpressible by drawing the viewer towards the sky 'to which the flag points and which the cross on the flag defines as the spiritual and Christian reality to which all earthly things are subject'.[114]

This may be too exclusive a reading, but the ineffable is certainly part of the painting's appeal. The poet Oehlenschläger, in fact, expressed his opinion that crude symbolism was too inflexible and akin to language, whereas nebulous symbolism was more potently poetic:

> A flag or a cathedral can stand for a concept. They are symbols of national and religious sentiment, which can never be adequately described in words. If the symbol's meaning could be exhausted verbally it would have no legitimacy ... the symbols of romanticism are self-sufficient. They can neither be translated or replaced.[115]

In a post-modern world Købke might be seen to deliberately leave the matter unresolved, something for the spectator to decide. A sublime nuance, however, had come more frequently to pervade his work and we know from letters of this time that he was suffering from a bout of his recurrent religious uncertainties. Issues of faith were also uppermost in his mind as he completed an altarpiece in the Zealand village of Ramløse, kept company with Freund, and admitted to Constantin Hansen in a letter of 28 December 1837: 'I am not a great lover of going out ... so I do not know much of what is going on in the art world.'[116]

During the winter of 1838 he worked on *Autumn Morning by the Sortedam Lake* [62], which again encompasses the lakeside and the transition between town and country. The spiritual loneliness conjured up by the single figure walking along the tow-path has led to the painting being compared to works by Friedrich, its genesis assumed to lie in Købke's introspection at this time.[117] The melancholy autumnal landscape and sense of seasonal decline is almost unique in Købke's oeuvre, finding company only with *Autumn Landscape with Frederiksborg Castle in the Middle Distance* [38] – two paintings that show changing seasons rather than the seeming permanence of summer.

Superficially there are features of these works that are shared with Friedrich, and also Dahl, and the latent effect of German romanticism seems undeniable. Characteristic works by Friedrich [60] reveal a similar use of emotive, subdued colour and melancholic overtones, whilst Dahl often draws on a vocabulary of bare trees evocatively silhouetted against bleak, dramatically lit landscapes, with distant buildings and wild birds [61]. However, the dissimilarities from the Dresden masters are also striking. Friedrich more than any artist imbued Nature with his own overtly spiritual ethos, but even tentative suggestions of this sort are rare in Købke's output. Even when the mood and light of his paintings are imbued with mildly transcendental overtones, they remain rooted in an earthly reality born of Eckersberg's teaching. Unlike Friedrich, Købke never 'invents' or stage-manages scenes drawn from imagination. He worked frequently in lyrical and poetic modes, but these were always based on analyses of the natural environment, never flights of the imagination, something of which, as Hannover averred, he was devoid.

In general, romantic landscape was concerned with mystical or religious experience, often fashioned from remote, primal or untouched vistas. Dahl most consistently does this in addressing the actual landscape through a romantic consciousness. Unlike Købke, he habitually worked on a large scale and depicted the land as a site of national heritage. This did influence Købke's younger colleagues, most notably Lundbye, but also Sødring. The dolmen stones included in Dahl's work [61], presumed to be ancient grave markers (though their function and date are still subject to debate) are utilised as markers of an ancient, heroic past which was being celebrated at the same time in nationalist poetry by writers such as Oehlenschläger. In this respect Dahl and his followers were essentially romantic naturalists, whereas Friedrich was an idealist. The works of both artists did have in common with Danish Golden Age art a perceived unity of man, nature and deity, but

60 · Caspar David Friedrich,
Raven Tree, c.1822
Louvre, Paris

61 · Johan Christian Dahl,
Winter Landscape near Vordingborg, 1829
Statens Museum for Kunst, Copenhagen

62 · *Autumn Morning by the Sortedam Lake*, 1838
Ny Carlsberg Glyptotek, Copenhagen

the outcome in Købke's case was a more earth-bound manifestation of the ideal, always grounded in a specific time and place. As has been tellingly noted of *Autumn Morning by the Sortedam Lake* [62], whilst the strange beauty of the misty autumnal day is realised with superb grace, 'the path along the lake leads to the Copenhagen suburb of Vesterbro, not to eternity'.[118]

This down-to-earth outlook also extended to Danish art criticism. Instead of observing aspects of the sublime in Købke's seeming romantic wanderer, the work was reviewed without any reference to gloomy or contemplative associations, but as a fresh, lively, natural scene, inviting the viewer to a brisk walk rather than to introspection.[119] The painting is not addressing symbolic or spiritual issues, but the temptation, nevertheless, to associate it with German romantic roots must be a recognition that behind a simple engagement with nature, a sense of a more permanent Ideal is being evoked. The natural world depicted may indeed be mutable and the seasons subject to change, but the source of its being, the Idea, is permanent, eternal and incorruptible.

The elegiac tone of *Autumn Morning by the Sortedam Lake* could also be interpreted as an ending since Købke left for Italy in August 1838, the year in which the work was exhibited at Charlottenborg, and did not return until he had completed his own two years of wandering. Købke did not subsequently go back to specifically Danish subjects in any of his finished works, yet the importance of Blegdammen and Dosseringen as inspiration for some of his most moving later creations remained, and he was again to make use of motifs drawn from these places at the end of his career.

Italy and the Return to Denmark ⤳

64 · *The Garden Gate of the Artist's Home on Blegdammen*, *c.*1841–5
Statens Museum for Kunst, Copenhagen

Whilst it had always been presumed that Købke would fall into line with his contemporaries and make the journey to Italy that was seen as obligatory for all aspiring artists, he continually prevaricated, and then only went reluctantly. Various reasons were found for delaying the trip, not least of which was the need for money from the Fund for the Public Benefit (Fonden Ad Usus Publicos), which provided funds for travelling scholarships. The fund, established by King Frederik V in 1765, supported science, literature and the arts, and in due course it awarded Købke a scholarship of 600 rigsdaler a year, a good, if not extravagant, sum.[120]

Yet nearly a year after the award, Købke was still dithering. In the middle of 1838, barely three weeks before his planned departure, he wrote to his sister Sophie, who was in Rome with her husband the artist F.C. Krohn, that he was cancelling his trip. Perhaps his newly-wed status deterred him at this point, but, unlike Krohn, he seems never to have considered taking Sanne with him, leaving an exasperated Sophie to write home: 'From Christen's last letter I see to my great amazement that he is not thinking of travelling, but do please tell me the reason??'[121]

Practicalities aside, it seems simply that Købke was disinclined to go on a prolonged trip, away from the comforts of home (and doubtless fearing the horrors of foreign cuisine), which others felt necessary – but about which he may have felt apprehensive or maybe just indifference. In an earlier letter from 1834 he had already confessed his lack of a spirit of adventure:

> ... *in this world my needs are simple. A nice little dwelling where one is comfortable and painters always know how to secure a place like this, and in addition a modest way of living when it comes to clothing and food, if just the world would leave one alone, so one is not disturbed when working, this is all I ask* ... [122]

These are clearly not the words of a soul imbued with wanderlust, yet Købke did eventually leave for Italy on 20 August 1838, on the insistence of Freund and with Krohn's persuasion. In this he at least showed more resolution than Friedrich, who never visited Rome despite the insistent invitation from Eckersberg's co-professor, J.L. Lund.[123] Købke was away, however, for little more than two years, which was a short period by comparison

65 · Constantin Hansen,
A Group of Danish Painters in Rome, 1837
Statens Museum for Kunst, Copenhagen

66 · Wilhelm Marstrand,
Portrait of the Painter Christen Købke, 1839
Statens Museum for Kunst, Copenhagen

with his peers. Thorvaldsen, exceptionally, remained in Rome for forty-one years, but Freund stayed for nearly eleven, Constantin Hansen for nine years, and Eckersberg spent six years in France and Italy. Most other artists remained abroad for more than two years, since the benefits of travel were deemed indispensable for completion of an artistic training. Rome swarmed with artists of many nationalities, and a small but considerable community of Danish painters was already stationed there. As was the case with other smaller nationalities, they tended to keep within their own orbit, fraternising with their German colleagues, but otherwise remaining isolated by their inability to speak Italian, as well as a degree of cultural diffidence. They fell back on a mutually supportive expatriate network and congregated at the Café Greco, near the Spanish Steps, where many waited for their travelling stipends to be forwarded. Købke fell into the same pattern, and once in Rome made straight for the comfort of the home of his sister Sophie and her husband. That sense of fraternal and rather cosy insularity is encapsulated in Hansen's celebrated image of Danish painters in Rome [65], of which Købke wrote to the artist admiringly when it was shipped back to Denmark for exhibition.[124] Few painters made it further than Italy where, like latter-day lotus eaters, many settled to a life of comfortable indolence until they were due to return. Martinus Rørbye was an exception, travelling in 1835 in the company of the architect Michael Gottlieb Bindesbøll to Athens and Turkey, places previously not visited by Danish artists. Hansen's painting shows the reclining Bindesbøll recounting their adventures. The artist Jørgen Sonne sits on the table to the right, whilst standing by him are the painters Albert Küchler and Ditlev Blunck. Leaning on the balcony railing is Wilhelm Marstrand, who gazes outwards. Hansen includes himself hatless, behind the speaker, whilst, seated against the shutter, Rørbye examines his coffee cup. It is a warm, down-to-earth image of comradeship in an alien environment, painted the year of Købke's wedding, and one could easily be tempted to imagine that the assembled artists are patiently awaiting his arrival.

Købke reached Rome in December 1838 after a long journey that had taken in Berlin, Dresden and Munich, and then on to Salzburg. In Italy he passed through Verona, Padua, Venice, Ferrara, Bologna, Ravenna, Mantua, Florence and, penultimately, Siena. Travel at this time was difficult and uncomfortable, largely made by unnerving carriage rides, but sometimes on foot (Købke walked from Siena to Rome, a distance on modern roads of 115 miles). It was also dangerous, so that artists travelled in pairs – Købke with the decorative painter Georg Christian Hilker. Marstrand's portrait of Købke [66] painted in 1839, depicts him with the customary beard and wide-brimmed hat which were thought to make travellers appear more formidable, although one doubts the efficacy in Købke's case.

In Rome, Købke was recurrently ill and between times was often nursing bedridden friends. He eased his financial position by undertaking portrait commissions since the scholarship money awarded in 1837 did not reach him until 1839. With the sun, his mood lifted in Italy, and whilst he told Høyen that he had hardly executed a single pencil stroke, he added that his time was being well used – by which he presumably meant he was observing and thinking.[125] In fact, he painted no finished works in Italy, but this was not uncommon. The purpose of travel was not necessarily to paint, but to look and record. A tour of the major Italian sites was a cultural expeditionary venture. The objective was to gather impressions and experiences and to assemble sufficient studies to act as an archive to be exploited in years to come as they were incorporated into finished paintings.

Købke's subsequent travels within Italy took him in 1839 through Naples, Capri and Pompeii in the company of Hansen. In Naples he copied Pompeian murals in the museum collection and sketched in the ruined city. He also paid close attention to his diet, and though he usually avoided fruit, he notes a passion for strawberries, an appetite which he indulged daily. In Capri he and Hansen seem to have let their hair down completely and Købke relates that they sang, danced and even helped to harvest and press the olives.[126] The pair went to Naples at Christmas and the following summer Købke returned to Pompeii where he completed studies for a later painting of the Forum [84] before, on 27 July 1840, leaving Naples for Denmark. They reached Copenhagen in September.

It has been customary to regard Købke's Italian sojourn as heralding a decline in his output – at least in his completed and exhibited works, those by which he was judged in the public arena, although that view has come to be reassessed. Attention has also been focused on his continued propensity when back in Denmark for sketching and executing works of a more personal nature, not destined for public display. It would be difficult to make the case, however, that the last phase of Købke's career matched the quality or assuredness of his earlier output. Nevertheless, there was a degree of practical, if not aesthetic, sense in Købke's inclination towards the production of larger, more finished and 'academic' Italian subjects. Exhibiting his proficiency with such scenes was vital if he was to prosecute his claim to being a 'serious' painter and thereby gain membership of the Academy. This conferred not merely status and livelihood, but brought fringe benefits which would give the artist and his family security, such as provision for a pension for widows and orphans. All of his completed works in the 1840s were on Italian themes derived from his travel archive, nearly all of which resulted in much needed sales, whilst one, *Rocky Coast, Capri, Soon after Sunrise*, became his second work to enter the royal collection.[127]

How to make use of his experiences in Italy was, however, only one problem amongst many that beset the artist on his return, and personal issues proved highly disruptive at this time. Whilst in Italy Købke suffered the death of his brother Hans Peter in 1839 and the following year the loss of Freund. His brother Carl died barely three months after his return, and in 1843 the death of his father caused financial difficulties. Two years later the Blegdammen home was sold and Købke moved into an apartment in the crowded city to fend financially for himself and his family. The resumption of his marriage, interrupted by his two-year absence, must also have required a degree of personal reorientation for the couple. In 1841 their first child, Peter, was born but postnatal complications kept Sanne bed-ridden. Writing to Constantin Hansen, who was still in Rome, Købke expressed his extreme concern for her survival, adding, 'That all this time I have only had little time to think of my own affairs goes without saying; for one and a half months I have been nursing unceasingly.'[128]

For all these reasons, the return to Denmark was an exceedingly testing time for the artist's fragile constitution and spiritual unease. The most crushing blow, however, came on 19 October 1846 when *View of Marina Piccola on Capri* [83] which he submitted in a bid to gain membership of the Academy was ignominiously rejected by ten votes to seven, with two abstentions. It is conjectured that Købke's failure to embrace the nationalism of a Danish subject got caught up in internal intrigues between the voting members. [129]

The work is not bad of its kind, but it is hardly that of a man whose horizons have been broadened by continental experience. Købke's earlier request for a two-year extension to the deadline for its submission, due in part to his father's death and the sale of the family home, meant there were six years between his return from Italy and the work's completion. There is a sense here, and in his other Italian themes, of an artist who has lost his individuality and vibrancy of touch. Although the works are technically proficient, it is as if Købke were trying to force himself into a manner to which he was not naturally suited. This shows particularly in the absence of the freshness and vitality of his Danish subjects, where he worked habitually in front of the motif. Købke seems to have been aware of this shortcoming, noting, 'I only wish that I had brought three times as many motifs with me home from Italy, as it will end up looking dry once I have completed what I have … '[130]

At this time Købke's letters suggest that he seriously considered a career as a decorative artist, which, if less prestigious, would have meant a more regular income. He had worked assiduously in Pompeii at copying ancient wall paintings and aspects of interior design, and in 1844 and 1845 he utilised this recently acquired familiarity with Italian murals to assist with the painting of the ornate ceilings in the Roman rooms of the Thorvaldsens Museum, then under construction. He also completed a ceiling decorated with vine leaves for the country residence of the merchant Hans Puggaard, and in 1846 proposed, though unsuccessfully, two imaginative designs for large wall decorations that would have given the house the air of a Roman villa.[131]

These intermittent commissions came to little, and, together with the occasional sale of an Italian scene, could hardly have provided a viable income. He nevertheless maintained a prodigious output and remained busy with family portraits, including some charming images of children, which, if inconsistent in terms of his previously irreproachable quality, were fine works. Chief amongst these is the unusually robust portrait of a relative, on his father's side, *Portrait of the Artist's Cousin's Son, P. Ryder* [67]. Ryder's sister Susanne had been married to Købke's late brother Carl, who had been a minister on the island of Bornholm until his death in 1840. Købke depicts the powerfully built figure in his work clothes, smoking a cigarillo with an assured gaze and confident pose, arms folded in a relaxed manner, as if resting at the end of a working day. Unusually for Købke, who normally included virtually no detail in the backgrounds of his portraits, he has situated his subject in his workplace and included a still life of a basket of pretzels behind the sitter. Completed in the year of the artist's death, it is amongst the more monumental of his portraits, and retains the finely controlled linear structure and carefully contrived finish of his very best works in this genre. Købke and Ryder appear to have shared speculative religious interests that occasioned a closeness between them. Writing to his sister Conradine in the spring of 1846, Købke (with his customary disregard for punctuation) commented upon Ryder in a manner that might have described himself: 'Poor Ryder is completely downhearted; God knows if he will ever be the same again, he is mulling over his place in the world and his conditions of life and it is ruining his body completely.'[132] However, there is none of

67 · Portrait of the Artist's Cousin's Son, P. Ryder, 1848
Private Collection

this anxiety in this compelling portrait of a man eminently at ease with himself, seated nonchalantly and gazing at the viewer with a look that is both kindly and imperturbable.

It is amongst the finest of Købke's portraits, and evidence that, at least where portraits were concerned, he had lost none of the understanding and technical accomplishment of his earlier works. The *Portrait of the Artist's Sister-in-Law, Johanne Elisabeth Købke, née Sundbye* [68] is at least as finely executed, and has a profundity hardly matched in any of his other portraits, even in what may be an unfinished state. It is an immensely subtle, yet direct, engagement with an individual whose delicate and sensitive inner being is implied in an entirely credible way. The painting is conceived in the simplest compositional terms, with just a hint of the obliquity favoured throughout his work, the colour subdued in a Whistler-like way, with the sitter's china blue/grey eyes intently focused on the artist – and whatever lay outside her. It is a painting that shows Købke's gifts entirely unimpaired when he was, as is clearly the case here, totally committed to his subject.

In these final years, Købke also continued his practice of making small, personal sketches and paintings close to the family home. *View of Dosseringen near Østerbro, Cloudy Sky* [69] is characteristic of these intimate works which allowed him freedom to be entirely himself, unhindered by academic precepts. As they do not seem to have been developed into more finished paintings they must be presumed to be autonomous works and not

70 · *View of Dosseringen towards Nørrebro, 1841–5*
Statens Museum for Kunst, Copenhagen

71 · *Study of Clouds over the Sea, 1840–5*
Statens Museum for Kunst, Copenhagen

preparatory studies. It is the engagement with the familiar that we have seen before: Købke has barely moved from his own garden gate and in the far distance we glimpse some of the houses that appear in the serene *View of a Street in Østerbro outside Copenhagen* of 1836 [57]. Here, however, the scene is rendered in deft and rapid strokes, the surface charged with a sense of the impending tempest. On a different day, in *View of Dosseringen towards Nørrebro* [70], he simply faces in the opposite direction to create a sparkling, hazy view of the lake, the footpath now running on the opposite side of the canvas. The vivacity of these small scenes, acutely observed on the spot, is in striking contrast to the laboriously concocted Italian works that display Købke's technical proficiency but lack any sense of vitality.

In these Dosseringen works there is more evidence of Købke's abiding interest in the sky, an ever mutable source of inspiration which dates back to his Citadel works – a legacy of Eckersberg.[133] Occasionally his depiction of a particular sky dominates the painting, while at other times it becomes the sole focus, as in, for example, *Study of Clouds over the Sea* [71]. Where previously Købke had simply included prominent cloud formations within his compositions as part of the type of realism inculcated by Eckersberg, he now concerned himself simply with this motif, as Constable, Friedrich and Dahl, amongst others, had done. The majority of these studies were of dramatic celestial unrest, the heavy black or grey cloud formations brooding and oppressive. Whether these and the freely painted, final Blegdammen landscapes speak of a progressive, even 'modern' enquiry into the very nature of painting, or whether they are the result of the death of the imagination, a 'manifestation of impotence',[134] can be endlessly debated. All that is certain is that Købke's will to work was undiminished, and that, at the end of his painting day, he was certainly home in time for dinner!

Perhaps fittingly, home itself was the last subject Købke would treat with the serenity and assurance that had marked his career. In 1845 he and his family moved to an apartment in Frederiksborggade, within the city, but as he prepared to leave the Blegdammen family home he set out, probably quite consciously, to memorialise it in four characteristically 'oblique' works. These paintings make no attempt to record the building, but rather to evoke the spirit of an intensely personal location. In fact, they show only those aspects of the house which relate to his and Sanne's home, not the entire family dwelling.

The painting known as *Garden Steps near the Artist's Studio on Blegdammen* [72], shows little more than Købke's own apartment, situated in the gable end of the building, which faced north-west, thereby giving him consistent light. The main elevation is glimpsed sharply foreshortened, but in bright sunshine which just catches the lower sections of the open studio doors. This sunlight also scintillates on the edges of the tree trunks on the other side of the garden fence, which itself, though in shadow, is lit in a similar way. A tree, the bright light flickering on its outer leaves, arches across the centre of the painting to the translucent area of sky. A serene and tender view of semi-rural domestic tranquillity, it shows the artist's powers undiminished.

All of these paintings include a gate, which, in three of them, stands open. Though the subject is so ordinary, it is difficult not to sense a universal symbolism, redolent of leave-taking and loss, nostalgia and memory. *The Garden Gate of the Artist's Home on Blegdammen* [64] is utterly simplified – brightly lit fence, leafy trees, the open gate leading on to the footpath, and a glimpse of Lake Sortedam. Only a tiny stretch of the lake is visible, but it is, of course, the place immortalised in so many of his greatest works. Framed by the open gate, a small sailing vessel, the reflection of its white sails on the water shimmering towards us, sails past a church on the opposite bank. Is it a potent symbol of voyaging and eternity, or only an aspect of the modern Copenhagen suburbs? Købke never overstates his meaning. It is certainly, however, a joyous and evocative work, and one that embodies

72 · *Garden Steps near the Artist's Studio on Blegdammen, c.1845*
Statens Museum for Kunst, Copenhagen

the twin concerns of Golden Age art, reality and the ideal, in a way that can be appreciated on both levels.

The last image of Købke, a drawing by P.C. Skovgaard, shows a wiser, more knowing individual than the young man in his early self-portrait [7]. By no means a spent force, the penetrating gaze is that of both a shrewd and engaging personality. He died on 7 February 1848, aged just thirty-seven, the cause being recorded as pneumonia, although his family held that his academic rejection was a contributory factor.[135] It has been speculated that his practice of the so-called 'Gräfenberg Cure', which involved copious cold baths and excessive water consumption, caused more harm than good, but Købke embraced it in the enthusiastic way that he had always sought remedies for his lifelong poor health. His funeral took place on 12 February in the Trinity Church, where Constantin Hansen sang a song especially written for the occasion, which included the verses:

> *For the last time we stay with you*
> *Our dear brother – The voice of psalm*
> *Will blend with the sighs of loss*
> *For your heart was of gold.*
> *In sorrow and in joy you appeared secure*
> *With faith, hope and of good cheer.*
>
> *The work of your Maker you contemplated with delight*
> *And you felt the strength and goodness of God*
> *When the glare of the sun was seen in the west*
> *When the tender bud was coming out;*
> *And many a picture from your hand*
> *Will bear witness of a loving spirit.*[136]

Købke was buried in Assistens Cemetery, where his grave can still be seen. He left behind him not only Sanne, but their six-year-old son Peter, and their two-year-old daughter Juliane Emilie. Sadly, just a year later, Sanne too died, and was buried close to her husband. The artist's sister, Sophie, took care of the children, and when she died in 1853 they remained with her husband F.C. Krohn, who, conveniently, and perhaps inevitably, remarried within the family, this time to Emilie Købke, Sanne's younger sister.

Following Købke's death and funeral, in December 1848, his belongings were auctioned off and his works dispersed, after which he was, largely, forgotten.[137] Even Høyen failed to commemorate his death, as he did with other artists, and it was as if by now this lost sheep of the nationalist cause was beyond the pale.

Afterword

Købke's resurrection as the greatest artistic talent of an age brimming with genius, waited until the late nineteenth century, when an exhibition of his works at the Fine Arts Society (Kunstforeningen) in 1884, followed by Hannover's pioneering biography of 1893, sparked a revival of interest. Købke's unerring eye and technical brilliance were reassessed, particularly in the light of his seeming to prefigure certain modern preoccupations, such as the elimination of literary anecdote or any overt story-telling. A contemporary audience was then more able to appreciate the subtlety and aesthetic autonomy of his works where the subject was essentially a vehicle for Købke to display his unrivalled powers of perception and the precision of his painterly technique. His choice of seemingly arbitrary viewpoints and use of unexpected fragments of his world as subject matter, had a radical originality which predated the less premeditated way in which the visual world would be treated by Impressionism, photography and Modernism generally.[138] As the twentieth century approached, he found a more receptive audience for his subtle and understated works than he had in his lifetime.

Købke stands, therefore, in a noble tradition of neglected talents whose work has been posthumously vindicated, but there is a striking dichotomy between the qualities that are now seen to be so important in his work and the view taken of the visual arts in his own lifetime. Despite the remarkable legacy of the Danish Golden Age artists, painting in Denmark in the first half of the nineteenth century lacked prestige. The intellectual Parnassus remained closed to them. Grundtvig, whose voice can hardly have been more influential at the time, ranked painting and sculpture 'as the lowest, most material forms of art', unlike literature and poetry, which partook of the mind, rather than the hand – a form of snobbery dating back to the ancient concept of the 'liberal arts', those fit for free men rather than the low or menial. Though fond of Thorvaldsen, *the* unrivalled artistic superstar of the age, Grundtvig made plain that he could not admire his work, believing God to be the only competent sculptor, and that there should be no intermediary.[139]

Kierkegaard was similarly dismissive of the artist's trade, as of the wider scientific field, believing that since God is the subject, He (and his creations) cannot be made the object of mankind or its investigations. He held that art is akin to death, in that preservation of the moment results in the extinction of the continuum that is life:

All art is essentially involved in a dialectical self-contradiction. The truly eternal cannot be painted or drawn or carved in stone, for it is spirit. But neither can the temporal … for when it is presented in these ways, it is presented eternally; every picture expresses a fixation of that particular moment. If I paint a man who is lifting a spoon to his mouth or blowing his nose, it is immediately eternalized – the man continues to blow his nose this one time as long as the painting endures.[140]

Købke did not, in fact, treat his subjects behaving in the transitory way that Kierkegaard describes, something more akin to genre painting. The result of intense personal contact with the subject of a portrait, or the momentary record of a place, are only able to contain the eternal when they are viewed by a consciousness that is aware of both the contingent and the eternal. A less extreme position is that of Sibbern, under whom Kierkegaard had studied, who believed that 'the spirituality of objects' could be represented in the way that the spirit can be revealed in the outward appearance of a face, and, by extension, in a representation of a face – as in Købke's finest portraits.[141]

Grundtvig's comments perhaps strike harder at an artist like Købke, in that whilst he aspired to depict the temporal in his art, he invoked through his work the eternal, that is, the divine, that underpinned life's phenomena. In that sense, he was indeed an intermediary, but perhaps more in the sense of being what Plato termed a *Poietic* painter, one whose contact with the divine does not seek to supplant the God-created original, but to transform it through a true understanding of the subject, rather than only grasp at its outward appearance.[142]

In this sense Købke's modesty and piety might be regarded as the vehicle of his legitimacy in an age of cultural snobbery and hierarchy. Whether one approached the divine intuitively or intellectually would not, ultimately, make any difference to the goal achieved. Købke's own comment that 'the Lord is strong in the weak'[143] indicates that he knew his limitations and attended first and foremost to the sphere he understood: the visual. In this he was dedicated to the development and exercise of his talent, rather than to theorising or giving written explanations. That he was construed either as an innocent or an unsullied conduit of his own innate talent, is attested by those around him who regarded his simplicity not in a pejorative sense, but as a token of honesty and sincerity. After his death, Købke's brother-in-law, Krohn, wrote in his obituary: 'He did not seek his objects in the world of make believe; his works are true reflections of his life and of the Nature which was close to him with no artificial additions.'[144] He did not mean by this that Købke never altered what he saw, but that his art was rooted in a spotless artistic integrity.

Hansen's funeral song has as its leitmotif Købke's goodness, his love of the works of creation and his faith in their maker. Expressing this in a different way, Lorenz Frølich identified Købke as the artist 'who has looked most happily, innocently, child-like at nature; that his eye in its purity also saw deepest … All loved him. Nothing impure could approach him.' The sculptor Jens Adolph Jerichau continued the theme: 'Who will deny *Købke* and others their deserts? Who is not attracted by what is innocent and true and kind?'[145]

Købke's own writings confirm his contemporaries' assessment of a straightforward and sincere personality, earnest in his desire to fulfil the potential of his talent, sustained by his religious outlook, but prone occasionally to self-doubt. His letters and journal entries show at times an abundance of spiritual speculation alternating with passages of dejection; but where Freund despaired of attaining perfection, Købke always saw light at the end of the tunnel, trusted in his belief, and settled for what he could achieve through his own efforts and God's grace. And in this he continually found solace. In an early letter to his sister Conradine he acknowledges this:

Completing a work only reminds me of my imperfection, but you can imagine how I thank God realising that this doesn't make me disheartened any more, instead it brings about an experience of clarity of what to do, and then I put my trust in God, that he will give me strength and good health to carry it through … this is what gives me contentment in life.[146]

It is tempting to speculate that this ingenuous outlook is what eventually nourished the public reassessment and appreciation of Købke's work – work that never seeks to impress or impose itself upon the viewer, never indulges in pompous or pretentious rhetoric, but, rather, quietly expects that its lasting virtues will in time be understood. The modesty and undisturbed simplicity of his output is doubtless a major part of his appeal to his many admirers today, but it should always be remembered that this pleasure is the result of profound formal skills that allow comparison with great predecessors like Vermeer or Chardin, who took the ordinary as their subject matter and imbued it with qualities that transcend the contingencies of time and place.

Nothing in Købke's background or training was remarkable or fundamentally different from that of many of his contemporaries. That he should emerge from Eckersberg's tutelage with a fully-formed aesthetic refinement has defied art historical analysis, and the essence of Købke's works remains to a degree ineffable. Ultimately, it may be necessary to concede to Købke his devout belief that his achievements rested on the agency of something inexpressible, and to which his sole obligation was to give of his best. Late in his short life he reiterated his simple credo, succinctly and eloquently, when he told his theologian brother-in-law Nicolai Feilberg:

I have given up making great demands on myself and think only according to my means of developing the gift the Lord has given me, and I do not set myself to do something in a couple of years, but for all the time we are here in this world, and then transfer it to the next; in that connection I have often thought of the words of the Apostle that one should be content with what one has, and from that spiritual point of view I think this is right.[147]

In Italy ～ KASPER MONRAD

74 · Detail from *View of the Bay of
Naples with Vesuvius in the Background*,
1839 [76]
Statens Museum for Kunst, Copenhagen

In August 1838 Købke left Denmark for his one and only foreign trip. In this way he fulfilled the expectations of the Royal Danish Academy of Fine Arts which, since its establishment in 1754, had an almost obligatory requirement that young artists should travel to Italy to study, especially to Rome. Unlike other artists who might spend from four to eight years in the southern part of Europe, Købke's Italian visit lasted only two years, and during this time he was in Rome for only five months. Later critics have therefore been reluctant to acknowledge the importance of his stay in Italy, although it has been generally agreed that the influence on his art was limited. Certainly, Købke's time in Italy was not as important to him as the time spent there by his teacher, Eckersberg, who was in Rome from 1813 to 1816.

Købke's first biographer, the art historian and critic Emil Hannover, did not think much of Købke's journey or its outcomes. He felt that Købke left 'without any particular [mental] baggage in any way at all', and further stated that he did not prepare for the event.[1] In his description of the Rome visit, Hannover – with undisguised amazement – gives the impression that Købke completely embraced the merry life of an artist by saying that 'He did not interrupt this state of well being for some time.'[2] Hannover clearly thought it was unfortunate that Købke – unlike many of his fellow artists – did not follow Eckersberg's example while he was in Rome. However, Hannover did acknowledge that during his stay in Naples and Capri Købke was quite industrious, but on balance he did not consider that the two years in Italy had been a positive experience.

Most art historians, who have since discussed Købke's Italian travels, agree with Hannover. It was not until the publication in 1996 of the three-volume work on the artist by Hans Edvard Nørregård-Nielsen, which contained a detailed biography of Købke, that there was a shift in this perception.[3] Nørregård-Nielsen included many quotations from letters, some from Købke himself, but also from other artists who were resident in Italy at around the same time. These highlight not only Købke's initial doubts on whether he should go abroad at all but also map out his stay in great detail. The writer also focuses on the many oil studies and drawings that Købke produced while in Italy. However, Nørregård-Nielsen still lent towards Hannover's critical assessment of the stay.[4] Købke's Italian travels, therefore, still require to be put in context.

It is true that it was not Eckersberg who provided Købke's guiding principle. Købke went to Italy with completely different intentions from those of his teacher. Contrary to the comments made by Hannover, Købke felt that he had prepared himself thoroughly prior to leaving Denmark and that the work he carried out during his time in Italy was done in a methodical manner. By looking in more detail at the preparations Købke made and by illustrating the work he produced while in Italy, it appears that Købke's Italian journey was more important to his art than has previously been recognised.

Hannover's expectations of Købke's Roman visit are in some ways quite understandable. Two very close fellow students and friends, Constantin Hansen and Jørgen Roed, who were in Italy at the same time as Købke, faithfully followed Eckersberg's example by producing architectural and picturesque views of Rome that showed the remains of antiquity. To a very great extent Eckersberg's small Roman works, which were based on thorough studies of nature and were completed in the open air, served as a model for the Academy students, and most young Danish artists travelling to Italy in the 1820s and 1830s very clearly saw this city through the eyes of their teacher. Ditlev Blunck who was not particularly close to Eckersberg wrote in 1829 from Rome to the Academy professor:

> *How often on all our excursions in this tremendous city do I find my thoughts turning to your friendly little drawing room in Charlottenborg Palace in Kongens Nytorv [in Copenhagen], where hang all the little pictures of Rome you painted here, and many times I have enjoyed seeking out the very places where you may have sat during your work, and especially now when every afternoon, almost without exception, I occupy myself in producing similar studies from nature.[5]*

It is possible that Købke saw Rome in the same light, but it is clear that he had not at any point planned to create a similar portfolio of studies. An indication of Købke's intentions while visiting Rome is contained in one of the few letters he sent from there. In spring 1839 Købke wrote to the art historian Niels Laurits Høyen and spoke about the plans he and his fellow travelling companion, the decorative painter Georg Christian Hilker, had:

> *I arrived here shortly before Christmas, and since then time has passed in looking at things, and I have to admit that I have scarcely done a single brush stroke, and yet I believe the time has not been wasted. I hardly expect I shall manage to start on anything now before I arrive in Naples, where Hilker and I are thinking of going after*

75 · *The Path up from Marina Piccola on Capri, c.1838*
Ny Carlsberg Glyptotek, Copenhagen

76 · *View of the Bay of Naples with Vesuvius in the Background*, 1839
Statens Museum for Kunst, Copenhagen

Easter. I am very much looking forward to the museum there. ... We could probably benefit if the Academy started a collection of copies ... of which we stand very much in need.[6]

Købke had, therefore, from early on in his trip made it clear that his destination was not Rome, but Naples and its surrounding area. There was more than one reason for this choice. He had become interested in decorative painting and was very much inspired by the sculptor Hermann Ernst Freund who hoped to revive mural painting inspired by antiquity and who wanted to combine the arts of painting, sculpture, functional art, furniture-making, decorative painting and architecture. The decoration of Freund's professorial accommodation was a most beautiful example of this. Consequently, Købke was interested in studying the Pompeian murals at the museum in Naples and during his stay there painted several copies of them.[7]

Another reason for choosing Naples over Rome was his own development as a painter. In the years prior to his trip, landscape painting had become increasingly important to Købke and there is no doubt that it was as a landscape painter and not as a painter of architecture that he left Denmark. In this respect, Eckersberg, who was particularly interested in architecture, was of limited importance to him, although the introduction to open air painting by his teacher during joint excursions in the Copenhagen area had influenced him a great deal.[8]

77 · *Castel dell'Ovo*
in Naples, 1839–40
Statens Museum for Kunst,
Copenhagen

Købke had to seek inspiration from other artists. Amongst Eckersberg's pupils only one was totally dedicated to landscape painting, namely Fritz Petzholdt. From 1830 to 1836 Petzholdt had resided almost permanently in Italy, painting in Sicily, Capri, and in the area near Olevano in the Roman Campagna. Prior to leaving Denmark, Købke took stock of the work of this painter who was only a couple of years older. He did this in a very forthright manner by copying two of Petzholdt's Capri works, a study and a more detailed painting, both of which depicted the Marina Piccola [75].[9] It is possible, therefore, that even before he arrived in Naples Købke had chosen this view of the natural harbour on the south side of the island as particularly important and had hoped to capture the special character of the scene by copying the paintings which Petzholdt had made there.

The landscapes around Naples, and not the least Capri, had at that time become popular with foreign artists, including some of the Danish painters who travelled to Italy after 1820[10] and Købke would have been aware of this. Although Petzholdt's importance to Købke is documented,[11] it has recently been suggested that the Norwegian landscape painter Thomas Fearnley, who was on Capri in 1833, also influenced him.[12] Fearnley was certainly closely connected to the Danish artistic community as he had studied in Copenhagen from 1821 to 1823 and also visited the city in 1827–8 and again in 1836. He influenced some of the Danish painters – for example, Martinus Rørbye.[13] Fearnley was well known for carrying a folder of his studies with him when travelling and he was always happy to show them to anyone interested in seeing them.[14] It is highly probable that Købke could have seen Fearnley's Capri studies when the artist was in Copenhagen in 1836. Their importance for Købke as an artist will be returned to later.

Although Købke based himself in Naples, he spent a great deal of time, and did most of his work on the neighbouring island of Capri. In Naples he made only a few studies in oil, but at the end of his stay he visited Pompeii several times where he worked on two studies and a number of related drawings. Two of the Naples studies could very well have been the first paintings he produced during his stay in Italy. In one of them Købke chose a popular scene showing the view across the Bay of Naples towards Vesuvius [76]. He depicts this from the water's edge on a hot, still, summer day, with everything bathed in sunlight and with the distant mountains hidden behind a heat haze. From this angle no perspective lines could direct the spectator's eyes into the background of the picture, and he had to create depth by using tonalitites of colour alone. This oil study was painted with light and flowing brush strokes although in several places comparatively wide strokes are clearly visible on the surface of the painting. At the same time, Købke also did a study of the famous medieval citadel Castel dell'Ovo with its excellent view of the harbour and the Naples coastline [77].[15] This fortified building looks like a massive sculpture but by depicting it bathed in strong sunlight, Købke diminishes its volume. He was very interested in this effect, and also in the reflections in the sea of the sky and of the building – including the variations in the intensity of the colour this created. From an artistic point of view the two studies are very similar to the studies Købke worked on immediately before he left Denmark.

At the end of September 1839 Købke and Constantin Hansen went to Capri and during three intense months Købke made many drawings and painted studies of this island. Købke was particularly interested in studies from Marina Piccola but unlike Petzholdt, whose works he had copied, he positioned himself to ensure that he had a wide view of the bay. In this Fearnley may have been a help to Købke as amongst the studies by the Norwegian painter one shows the majestic mountain Monte Castiglione, the marina itself and part of the Neapolitan gulf with the hill Punta Tragara and the reefs I Faraglioni [78].[16] Købke, following Fearnley's example, tried to capture the special character of the whole of the southern coastal area for three large compositions, which he planned to produce when he returned to Copenhagen. The paintings were to show this picturesque area from slightly staggered angles. In two of them he has left Monte Castiglione as the compositional point of reference, with the marina appearing in one of them. In the third work, the marina is the main focus of the painting but seen from a point which is higher and further away than the view depicted by Petzholdt.

Købke also made several large compositional drawings and some detailed studies, as well as studies in oil and he planned his work to ensure that the various preliminary works would augment one another. Although the two finished works of Monte Castiglione show almost identical scenes, Købke still produced compositional drawings for both of them, including *View of Marina Piccola on Capri* [79]. These differ from his previous drawings as they record not only the composition but also minute details such as the rock formations and grassy areas and the distribution of light and shade which would be an essential aid to Købke when working on the painting. As he had planned to produce one of the scenes

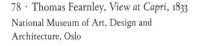

78 · Thomas Fearnley, *View at Capri*, 1833
National Museum of Art, Design and Architecture, Oslo

79 · *View of Marina Piccola on Capri*, 1839
Department of Prints and Drawings, Statens Museum for Kunst, Copenhagen

80 · *Marina Piccola, Capri*, 1839
Museum of Fine Arts, Boston, Gift of John
Goelet in honour of Perry T. Rathbone

81 · *View of Marina Piccola on Capri*, 1839
Göteborgs Konstmuseum, Gothenburg

bathed in the morning light and the other one in the afternoon sun, he had to consider the changes in the shadows in each of the two compositions. He therefore made two almost identical compositional drawings for the two paintings, which differ primarily in the distribution of light and shadow.

In the studies in oil it was of course the light and the play of colour that he wished to capture. It is very obvious that the two paintings are complementary. One shows the total composition from a distance [81], while the other focuses more closely on details such as the rock formation at the water's edge [80]. In these studies Købke has painted using a much lighter method and with wider brush strokes than he did before he left Denmark. While previously there was no clear artistic difference between the smaller finished paintings and the preliminary studies for them, Købke's studies are now more sketch-like. The same trend can be seen in an unfinished study of the surf on the Capri coast [85]. Although the coastal area is clearly incomplete, the waves and the breakers against the cliffs have been painted with what was for Købke a newly acquired virtuosity, which is also seen in the waves in the study *Rough Sea on a Rocky Coast* [86]. It seems that the stay in Capri allowed Købke greater artistic freedom, and it is very possible that Fearnley could have inspired Købke in this manner of painting. One of Fearnley's oil sketches, *Study of Cliffs on Capri*, is a detailed study of the coastal area of Capri and there are clear parallels as regards the angle and style of painting in the work of the two artists [82].[17] Perhaps the Norwegian helped Købke to open his eyes to a painterly solution that was different from the detailed painting style practised by Eckersberg. The similarities in the views selected by both Fearnley and Købke for their Capri oil studies include the unusual feature, the so-called Arco Naturale on the eastern part of the island.[18]

On his return from Capri Købke went to Naples where he energetically copied the antique murals in the museum. Towards the end of his stay he decided to go to Pompeii. He spent only three days in total in this ancient town but as the stays are well documented, it is possible to see how carefully he selected the motifs and planned his work. During these days he worked intensely and completed the necessary studies which he would use to produce two larger works. On 24 June 1840 he chose the scene for a painting of the gate at Via Sepulcralis and produced a compositional drawing. Just over a week later, on 3 July, he returned to Pompeii and produced an oil study of the scene.[19] He had by then already planned how to use this in a larger painting, as on the same day he did a detailed drawing of an overgrown block of stone from one of the ruins as a supplement to the compositional drawing and the oil study in order to include it in the final painting.[20] At this time he must have chosen the scene for another composition, as on his third and final visit on 10 July he

82 · Thomas Fearnley, *Study of Cliffs on Capri*, 1833
National Museum of Art, Architecture and Design, Oslo

83 · *View of Marina Piccola on Capri*, 1846
Private Collection

did a compositional drawing and the oil study for a painting of the Forum in Pompeii [84], and probably two detailed drawings, both undated.[21]

The oil study of the Forum in Pompeii is particularly remarkable considering how little time Købke spent on it. He painted it in just one day without making any alterations. The work, which is a study of astounding richness of detail, is characterised by a beautiful sense of light and atmosphere. The scene itself is at the same time both obvious and unusual. Købke chose the central part of the town, but has placed himself to ensure that one single column is the focal point of the work. From this angle the Forum, which had been planned according to a clear and logical structure, seemed almost chaotic, and the overall sense of the locality is lost.

On 27 July 1840 Køble left Naples to return to Denmark. The new artistic freedom he had found in Italy did not show in the larger paintings that he produced from his Italian studies, but can be seen in the smaller, unpretentious studies which he painted in the open air near his home and which are markedly different from the work he was producing before he left Denmark.

Previous books and articles on Købke have never recognised the benefits of his travels to Italy, although one authority on his art has acknowledged it, the artist's great-nephew, Mario Krohn. As they had remained in the family, Krohn grew up with, and inherited, many of Købke's works. His father Pietro Krohn had arranged the first Købke exhibition in 1884, and in 1912 Mario himself put on a large retrospective of the artist's works. Three years later he published the still authoritative catalogue of Købke's paintings, and he has with convincing precision dated all the Danish oil studies before or after the trip to Italy.[22] Unfortunately, he did not publish his arguments for the dates of the works, and it was not until the important retrospective in 1996 that it was possible to re-evaluate how significant Købke's journey to Italy really was.[23]

People in Købke's World

Peter Berendt Købke
1771–1843 *Købke's father*

Cecilia Margrete Købke
1778–1867 *Købke's mother*

Susanne Cecilie Købke, née Købke
1810–1849 *Købke's wife; married 1837*

Hans Peter Carl Købke
1841–1923 *Købke's son*

Juliane Emilie Købke
1845–1927 *Købke's daughter*

DANISH ARTISTS

Nicolai Abraham Abildgaard
1743–1809 *Painter*

Wilhelm Bendz
1804–1832 *Painter*

Ditlev Blunck
1798–1854 *Painter*

Dankvart Dreyer
1816–1852 *Painter*

Christoffer Wilhelm Eckersberg
1783–1853 *Painter; Købke's tutor*

Hermann Ernst Freund
1786–1840 *Sculptor*

Lorenz Frølich
1820–1908 *Painter, etcher, illustrator*

C.D. Gebauer
1777–1831 *Animal painter*

Constantin Hansen
1804–1880 *Painter*

Georg Christian Hilker
1807–1875 *Decorative painter*

Christian Holm
1803–1846 *Animal painter*

Christian Albrecht Jensen
1792–1870 *Portrait painter*

Jens Adolph Jerichau
1816–1883 *Sculptor*

Jens Juel
1745–1802 *Painter*

F.C. Krohn
1806–1883 *Sculptor; Købke's brother-in-law*

C.A. Lorentzen
1746–1828 *Painter; Købke's tutor*

J.L. Lund
1777–1867 *Painter*

Johan Thomas Lundbye
1818–1848 *Painter, illustrator*

Wilhelm Marstrand
1810–1873 *Painter*

Fritz Petzholdt
1805–1838 *Painter*

Jørgen Roed
1808–1888 *Painter*

Martinus Rørbye
1803–1848 *Painter*

P.C. Skovgaard
1817–1875 *Painter*

Frederik Sødring
1809–1862 *Painter*

Jørgen Sonne
1801–1890 *Painter*

Bertel Thorvaldsen
1770–1844 *Sculptor*

DANISH CULTURAL FIGURES

Hans Christian Andersen
1805–1875 *Author and poet*

Steen Steensen Blicher
1782–1848 *Author and poet*

August Bournonville
1805–1879 *Choreographer and ballet master*

Nikolai Frederik Severin Grundtvig
1783–1872 *Theologian, poet, historian*

Emil Hannover
1864–1923 *Art historian; Købke's first biographer*

Niels Laurits Høyen
1798–1870 *Art historian and critic*

B.S. Ingemann
1789–1862 *Romantic novelist*

Søren Kierkegaard
1813–1855 *Philosopher and theologian*

Finn Magnusen
1781–1847 *Archaeologist*

Adam Oehlenschläger
1779–1850 *Poet and playwright*

Hans Christian Ørsted
1777–1851 *Physicist, chemist, poet*

Joachim Frederik Schouw
1789–1852 *Botanist*

F.C. Sibbern
1785–1872 *Philosopher, novelist, poet*

Chronology ~

1754 The Royal Danish Academy of Fine Arts is founded by Frederik V.

1801 The Danish navy is crushed by Lord Nelson at the Battle of Copenhagen.

1807 The British bombardment destroys large parts of Copenhagen and the Danish fleet is handed over to the British army.

1808 Frederik VI is proclaimed King of Denmark and Norway.

1810 Christen Schjellerup Købke is born on 26 May 1810. He is the son of master baker Peter Berendt Købke and his wife Cecilia Margrete and the fifth of eleven children.

1813 The Danish State is declared bankrupt.

1814 Following the Napoleonic Wars and the Treaty of Kiel, Norway, which is part of the Danish Kingdom, is handed over to Sweden.

1815 The Købke family move to Frederiksborg (today called Hillerød), a village twenty miles north of Copenhagen.

1818 Købke's father is appointed master baker to the military Citadel just outside the ramparts of Copenhagen.

1819 The Købke family move to the Citadel where they live for the next fourteen years.

1822 Købke enters the Royal Danish Academy of Fine Arts at Charlottenborg Palace.

1825 The Fine Arts Society (Kunstforeningen) is established by the influential art historian N.L. Høyen and the painter and Academy professor C.W. Eckersberg.

1826 After passing through the obligatory classes at the Academy, Købke becomes a student of the eighty-year-old painter C.A. Lorentzen.

1827 The royal collection at Christiansborg Palace opens to the public.

1828 After the death of Lorentzen, Købke studies under C.W. Eckersberg.

1829 Købke spends the summer in Århus in Jutland visiting friends. The sculptor Hermann Ernst Freund returns from Italy and is appointed professor at the Academy. N.L. Høyen is appointed professor of history and mythology.

1830 Købke finishes *The Transept of Århus Cathedral* [31] and paints *View of the Plaster Cast Collection at Charlottenborg* [8]. The Fine Arts Society buys both paintings in 1831.

1831 Købke's debut at the spring exhibition at Charlottenborg. The Academy awards him the small silver medal. The four works on display are *The Transept of Århus Cathedral* [31], *View of the Plaster Cast Collection at Charlottenborg* [8], *View of the Square in the Citadel Looking towards the Citadel Ramparts* [20] and *The Cigar Seller at the Northern Exit from the Citadel* [26]. During the summer Købke spends time in Frederiksborg where he meets Høyen whose praise of Frederiksborg Castle as 'the finest castle in northern Europe' encourages Købke to paint the monument.

1832 Købke is awarded the large silver medal. Together with his friend, the painter Frederik Sødring, Købke rents a studio in Toldbodvej, close to the Citadel, where he paints his friend's portrait [46]. Other portraits painted in this year are *Portrait of Inger Margrethe Høyen* [42] and *Portrait of an Old Peasant Woman* [49].

1833 Købke concludes his formal training at the Academy around 1832–3. Købke's father retires and the family moves from the Citadel to a large house situated between Blegdammen and Lake Sortedam. Købke sets up a studio in one end of the house. In October he completes his only self-portrait [1].

1834 Købke receives his first commission from the Fine Arts Society (Kunstforeningen) and paints *View outside the North Gate of the Citadel* [27]. He begins the decorative scheme of the dining room in his parents' new home.

1835 Kølbke stays at Frederiksborg from August to October where he paints *Frederiksborg Castle in the Evening Light* [37] as a response to a competition arranged by the Fine Arts Society.

1836 Kølbke completes *View of a Street in Østerbro, outside Copenhagen* [57] showing one of the main roads leading in to Copenhagen. Kølbke is engaged to his cousin Susanne Cecilie Købke.

1837 Købke paints *The Northern Drawbridge to the Citadel in Copenhagen* [28]. In the autumn he travels with Freund to the island of Bornholm. On 7 November he marries Susanne.

1838 Købke paints *View from Dosseringen near the Sortedam Lake Looking towards Nørrebro* [58] and begins work on the monumental *Portrait of the Sculptor Hermann Ernst Freund* [52]. He also completes an altarpiece, a commissioned work for Ramløse Church with the subject of *Christ and Nicodemus*. On 20 August Købke leaves for Italy on a two-year scholarship in the company of the decorative artist G.C. Hilker. They spend several months travelling through Germany, Austria and Italy before arriving in Rome on 8 December.

1839 In May Købke travels to Naples with Hilker, Constantin Hansen, and Just Jerndorff. Hansen and Købke leave Naples for Capri and stay there from September until December. On his return to Naples, Købke receives news that his younger brother Hans Peter Købke has died. The royal collection buys Købke's *View from Dosseringen near the Sortedam Lake Looking towards Nørrebro* [58]. In 1839 Christian VIII is proclaimed King of Denmark and reigns until his death in 1848.

1840 Købke returns to Pompeii in June and July where he draws and paints sketches of the ancient ruins. The news of Freund's death on 30 June reaches Hansen and Købke at the end of July. On 27 July Købke leaves Naples for Rome where he stays only a few days before travelling back to Denmark, arriving on 24 September. Later in the year his brother Carl Købke dies.

1841 Susanne becomes seriously ill after the birth of their first child Hans Peter Carl in June. In the autumn the Fine Arts Society commissions the painting *View of the Forum in Pompeii* [84]. Købke paints a series of more personal works showing the area of the Blegdammen home and Lake Sortedam [64, 69, 70, 72].

1842 The Royal Danish Academy accepts Købke's proposal of a Capri subject as his membership piece. According to Academy rules the painting must be completed within two years.

1843 Købke's father dies.

1844 Købke assists in the classical decoration of the ceilings of the newly built Thorvaldsens Museum. He receives an extension of two years to complete his membership piece.

1845 Købke and Susanne's second child Juliane Emilie is born. The house at Blegdammen is sold. Købke moves with Susanne and their two children to an apartment located inside the ramparts.

1846 Købke completes his submission to gain membership of the Academy, *View of Marina Piccola on Capri* [83], but the work is rejected.

1848 On 7 February Købke dies of pneumonia and on 12 February he is buried in Assistens Cemetery in Copenhagen. In December an auction of Købke's paintings and oil studies is held and a large part of his work is bought by fellow artists.

1849 Susanne Købke dies and her two children are left in the care of Sophie, Købke's sister. The absolute monarchy is abolished and parliamentary democracy is established.

1884 The first exhibition of Købke's paintings is held at the Fine Arts Society.

SK

Exhibition Checklist ⁓

This list features the works that are included in the exhibition. It is arranged in five sections with the works in chronological order.

CHARLOTTENBORG

View of the Plaster Cast Collection at Charlottenborg, 1830
Oil on canvas · 41.5 × 36cm
The Hirschsprung Collection, Copenhagen
[plate 8]

The Transept of Århus Cathedral, 1830
Oil on canvas · 48.5 × 34cm
Statens Museum for Kunst, Copenhagen
[plate 31]

Nude Figure. Sitting Boy, 1833
Oil on canvas · 58.3 × 48.7cm
Statens Museum for Kunst, Copenhagen
[plate 15]

Male Nude, 1833
Oil on canvas · 54 × 44cm
The Royal Danish Academy of Fine Arts, Copenhagen
[plate 16]

THE CITADEL

Cigar Seller at the Northern Exit from the Citadel, 1830
Oil on canvas · 23 × 25cm
Musée du Louvre, Paris
[plate 26]

View from the Loft of the Grain Store at the Bakery in the Citadel, 1831
Oil on canvas · 39 × 30.5cm
Statens Museum for Kunst, Copenhagen
[plates 22 and 73]

View of the Square in the Citadel Looking towards the Citadel Ramparts, c.1831
Oil on canvas · 30 × 23.4cm
National Gallery of Scotland, Edinburgh
Bought 1989 with assistance from The Art Fund
[plate 20]

View of the Citadel Ramparts towards Langelinie and the Naval Harbour, c.1832
Oil on canvas · 23.3 × 33cm
Statens Museum for Kunst, Copenhagen
[plate 23]

View of the Courtyard near the Bakery in the Citadel, c.1832
Oil on canvas · 33 × 24cm
Ny Carlsberg Glyptotek, Copenhagen
[plate 21]

View from a Window in Toldbodvej Looking towards the Citadel, c.1833
Oil on paper on canvas · 15 × 27.5cm
Statens Museum for Kunst, Copenhagen
[plate 25]

View from the Citadel Ramparts across the Moat and Langelinie towards the Limekiln, c.1833
Oil on canvas · 23.5 × 33.5cm
Ordrupgaard, Copenhagen
[plate 24]

View Outside the North Gate of the Citadel, 1834
Oil on canvas · 79 × 93cm
Ny Carlsberg Glyptotek, Copenhagen
[plate 27]

The Northern Drawbridge to the Citadel in Copenhagen, 1837
Oil on canvas · 44.2 × 65.1cm
The National Gallery, London
[plates 18 and 28]

FREDERIKSBORG

One of the Small Towers on Frederiksborg Castle, c.1834
Oil on canvas · 25.5 × 18.5cm
The David Collection, Copenhagen
[plate 33]

Roof Ridge of Frederiksborg Castle, with View of Lake, Town and Forest, c.1834–5
Oil on canvas · 177 × 171cm
Det danske Kunstindustrimuseum (Danish Museum of Art & Design), Copenhagen
[plate 34]

Frederiksborg Castle in the Evening Light, 1835
Oil on canvas · 71.8 × 103.4cm
The Hirschsprung Collection, Copenhagen
[plates 29 and 37]

Frederiksborg Castle. View near the Møntbro Bridge, 1836
Oil on canvas · 58 × 64cm
Statens Museum for Kunst, Copenhagen
[plate 36]

PORTRAITS

Portrait of the Artist's Mother, Cecilia Margrete, née Petersen, 1829
Oil on canvas · 23.5 × 19.5cm
National Gallery of Scotland, Edinburgh
[plate 4]

Portrait of Wilhelm Bendz, c.1830
Oil on canvas · 22 × 19cm
The National Gallery, London

Ida Thiele, the Future Mrs Wilde as a Child, 1832
Oil on canvas · 22.5 × 20cm
Statens Museum for Kunst, Copenhagen
[plate 45]

Portrait of Inger Margrethe Høyen, née Schrøder. The Art Historian N.L. Høyen's Mother, 1832
Oil on canvas · 30.5 × 25cm
Statens Museum for Kunst, Copenhagen
[plate 42]

Portrait of the Landscape Painter Frederik Sødring, 1832
Oil on canvas · 42.2 × 37.9cm
The Hirschsprung Collection, Copenhagen
[plate 46]

Portrait of an Old Peasant Woman, 1832
Oil on canvas · 30.5 × 26.5cm
Randers Kunstmuseum, Randers
[plate 49]

Portrait of an Old Sailor, 1832
Oil on canvas · 31 × 27cm
Statens Museum for Kunst, Copenhagen
[plate 50]

Portrait of the Artist's Cousin and Brother-in-Law, the Grocer Christian Petersen, c.1833
Oil on canvas · 31.5 × 27cm
Statens Museum for Kunst, Copenhagen

Self-portrait, c.1833
Oil on canvas · 42 × 35.5cm
Statens Museum for Kunst, Copenhagen
[plate 1]

Portrait of the Animal Painter Christian Holm, 1834
Oil on canvas · 26 × 20.2cm
Statens Museum for Kunst, Copenhagen
[plate 48]

Portrait of the Merchant Andreas Reiersen, 1834
Oil on canvas · 30.5 × 23cm
Ordrupgaard, Copenhagen

Portrait of the Naval Lieutenant D. Christen Schifter Feilberg, c.1834
Oil on canvas · 52.5 × 37.5cm
Statens Museum for Kunst, Copenhagen
[plate 47]

Portrait of the Artist's Father, Master Baker Peter Berendt Købke, c.1835
Oil on canvas · 23.4 × 19.9cm
Statens Museum for Kunst, Copenhagen
[plate 5]

*Portrait of the Artist's Wife, Susanne
Cecilie Købke, née Købke, c.1836*
Oil on canvas · 73.5 × 57.6cm
Statens Museum for Kunst, Copenhagen
[plate 51]

*Portrait of the Painter Wilhelm
Marstrand, 1836*
Oil on canvas · 18.5 × 15cm
Statens Museum for Kunst, Copenhagen
[plate 39]

*Portrait of the Sculptor Hermann
Ernst Freund, c.1838*
Oil on canvas · 158 × 96cm
The Royal Danish Academy of Fine Arts,
Copenhagen
[plate 52]

*Portrait of the Artist's Sister-in-Law,
Johanne Elisabeth Købke, née Sundbye,
c.1842*
Oil on canvas · 28.5 × 21cm
Statens Museum for Kunst, Copenhagen
[plate 68]

*Portrait of the Artist's Cousin's Son,
P. Ryder, 1848*
Oil on canvas · 74.5 × 53.5cm
Private Collection
[plate 67]

BLEGDAMMEN
AND LAKE SORTEDAM

*View of a Street in Østerbro outside
Copenhagen. On the Right 'Rosendal',
in the Background 'Petersborg', 1836*
Oil on canvas · 106.5 × 161.5cm
Statens Museum for Kunst, Copenhagen
[plate 57]

*View from the Limekiln with
Copenhagen in the Background, 1836*
Oil on canvas · 34 × 55cm
Nivaagaards Malerisamling / Nivaagaard
Picture Gallery Collection, Nivå
[plate 56]

*View of Dosseringen. In the Foreground
a Group of Reeds, c.1837*
Oil on paper on canvas · 24.2 × 27.8cm
Ordrupgaard, Copenhagen
[plate 63]

*View from Dosseringen near the
Sortedam Lake Looking towards
Nørrebro, c.1838*
Oil on canvas · 53 × 71.5cm
Statens Museum for Kunst, Copenhagen
[plates 53 and 58]

Study of Clouds over the Sea, 1840–5
Oil on paper on canvas · 15 × 21.5cm
Statens Museum for Kunst, Copenhagen
[plate 71]

*View of Dosseringen near Østerbro,
Cloudy Sky, 1841–5*
Oil on paper on cardboard · 22 × 29.5cm
Statens Museum for Kunst, Copenhagen
[plate 69]

*View of Dosseringen towards Nørrebro,
1841–5*
Oil on paper on canvas · 22 × 30cm
Statens Museum for Kunst, Copenhagen
[plate 70]

*The Garden Gate of the Artist's Home
on Blegdammen, c.1841–5*
Oil on paper on canvas · 29.5 × 24.5cm
Statens Museum for Kunst, Copenhagen
[plate 64]

*Garden Steps near the Artist's Studio
on Blegdammen, c.1845*
Oil on paper on canvas · 22.5 × 33cm
Statens Museum for Kunst, Copenhagen
[plate 72]

ITALY

Rough Sea on a Rocky Coast, 1839
Oil on paper on canvas · 27.1 × 38.8cm
Statens Museum for Kunst, Copenhagen
[plate 86]

*View of the Bay of Naples with
Vesuvius in the Background, 1839*
Oil on paper on canvas · 24.9 × 35cm
Statens Museum for Kunst, Copenhagen
[plates 74 and 76]

Castel dell'Ovo in Naples, 1839–40
Oil on paper on canvas · 25 × 36cm
Statens Museum for Kunst, Copenhagen
[plate 77]

Rough Sea, Capri Study, 1839–40
Oil on paper on canvas · 27.5 × 39.5cm
Ordrupgaard, Copenhagen
[plate 85)

Select Bibliography

AMSTERDAM AND COPENHAGEN 2001
Lene Bøgh Rønberg, et al., *Two Golden
Ages: Masterpieces of Dutch and
Danish Painting*, exhibition catalogue,
Rijksmuseum, Amsterdam and Statens
Museum for Kunst, Copenhagen 2001

ANDERBERG 1999
Birgitte Anderberg, et al., *Ordrupgaard.
Danish Art from the Century of the Golden
Age*, Charlottenlund 1999

BENCARD 2000
Mogens Bencard (ed.), *Intersections. Art
and Science in the Golden Age*, Copenhagen
2000

BERMAN 2007
Patricia G. Berman, *In Another Light:
Danish Painting in the Nineteenth Century*,
London 2007

BRAMSEN 1994
Henrik Bramsen, *Fra rokoko til guldalder.
Ny dansk kunsthistorie*. vol.3 (ed. Peter
Michael Hornung), Copenhagen 1994

COPENHAGEN 1981
Hans Edvard Nørregård-Nielsen, *Købke og
Kastellet. Et dansk guldaldermotiv*, exhi-
bition catalogue, Ny Carlsberg Glyptotek,
Copenhagen 1981

COPENHAGEN 1994
Annette Johansen, et al., *Den nøgne
guldalder. Modelbilleder C.W. Eckersberg
og hans elever*, exhibition catalogue, Den
Hirschsprungske Samling, Copenhagen
1994 (summary in English)

COPENHAGEN 1996
Hans Edvard Nørregård-Nielsen, Kasper
Monrad (eds.), *Christen Købke 1810–1848*,
exhibition catalogue, Statens Museum for
Kunst, Copenhagen 1996

GUNNARSSON 1998
Torsten Gunnarsson, *Nordic Landscape
Painting in the Nineteenth Century*,
Newhaven and London 1998

HANNOVER 1893
Emil Hannover, *Maleren Christen Købke. En
studie i Dansk Kunsthistorie*, Copenhagen
1893

JACOBSEN 2000
Helge Seidelin Jacobsen, *An Outline History
of Denmark*, Copenhagen 2000

JESPERSEN 2004
Knud J.V. Jespersen, *A History of Denmark*,
Basingstoke 2004

KENT 1993
Neil Kent, 'Christen Købke's drawings.
Assessing a little-known master', *Apollo*,
March 1993, pp.175–7

KJØRUP 1997
Søren Kjørup, 'Twins: Købke's Portrait
of Sødring', *Statens Museum for Kunst
Journal*, vol.1, 1997, pp. 42–59

KØBKE 1848
Auction catalogue of Købke's work
following his death. *Fortegnelse over
afdøde C.S. Köbkes efterladte Samling af
Oliemalerier, Studier, Haandtegninger,
Raderinger, Kobbere især Portraiter, og 3
raderede Kobberplader, hvilke bortsælges

ved offentlig Auction Mandagen den 18de
December 1848 om Formiddagen kl. 9 og
følgende Dage*, Copenhagen 1848

KROHN 1915
Mario Krohn, *Maleren Christen Købkes
Arbejder*, Copenhagen 1915

LINNET 2001
Ragni Linnet, 'An Art of Blindness.
Kierkegaard and the Nature of Pictures',
Nordisk Estetisk Tidskrift, 23, 2001,
pp.63–81

LINNET 2003
Ragni Linnet, 'Golden Tears: Johan Thomas
Lundbye and Søren Kierkegaard', in
Jon Stewart (ed.), *Kierkegaard and His
Contemporaries: The Culture of Golden
Age Denmark*, Berlin and New York 2003,
pp.406–26

LONDON 1984
Kasper Monrad, et al., *Danish Painting:
The Golden Age*, exhibition catalogue, The
National Gallery, London 1984

LOS ANGELES, NEW YORK, AND
COPENHAGEN 1993–4
Kasper Monrad, et al., *The Golden Age
of Danish Painting*, exhibition catalogue,
Los Angeles County Museum of Art,
The Metropolitan Museum of Art, New
York, and the Statens Museum for Kunst,
Copenhagen 1993–4

MONRAD 1994
Kasper Monrad, *Dansk Guldalder.
Hovedværker på Statens Musem for Kunst*,
Copenhagen 1994

MONRAD 2002
Kasper Monrad, 'Italian Rocks. Plein-air Studies by neglected Danish Painters from the Early 19th Century, *Statens Museum for Kunst Journal*, vol.6, 2002, pp.6–23

MONRAD 2006
Kasper Monrad, et al., 'Hidden Drawings from the Danish Golden Age. Drawing and Underdrawing in Danish Golden Age Views from Italy', *SMK Art Journal*, 2006, pp.111–19

NEW YORK, PITTSBURGH, AND SACRAMENTO 1995–6
Hans Edvard Nørregård-Nielsen, *The Golden Age of Danish Art: Drawings from the Royal Museum of Fine Arts, Copenhagen*, exhibition catalogue, The Frick Collection, New York, The Frick Art Museum, Pittsburgh, and the Crocker Art Museum, Sacramento 1995–6

NØRREGÅRD-NIELSEN 1980
Hans Edvard Nørregård-Nielsen, *Guldaldermaleren Christen Købke*, Copenhagen 1980

NØRREGÅRD-NIELSEN 1981
Hans Edvard Nørregård-Nielsen, 'The Lyricism of Christen Købke', *Apollo*, June 1981, pp.372–3

NØRREGÅRD-NIELSEN 1991
Hans Edvard Nørregård-Nielsen, *Undervejs med Christen Købke*, Copenhagen 1991

NØRREGÅRD-NIELSEN 1995
Hans Edvard Nørregård-Nielsen, *Danish Painting of the Golden Age*, Ny Carlsberg Glyptotek, Copenhagen 1995

NØRREGÅRD-NIELSEN 1996
Hans Edvard Nørregård-Nielsen, *Christen Købke*, 3 vols, Copenhagen 1996

NØRREGÅRD-NIELSEN 2006
Hans Edvard Nørregård-Nielsen, *Christen Købke*, Copenhagen 2006

OTTAWA, HAMBURG, AND COPENHAGEN 1999–2000
Catherine Johnston (ed.), *Baltic Light: Early Open-Air Painting in Denmark and North Germany*, exhibition catalogue, National Gallery of Canada, Ottawa, Hamburger Kunsthalle, and Thorvaldsens Museum, Copenhagen 1999–2000

POULSEN 1976
Vagn Poulsen, *Danish Painting and Sculpture*, Copenhagen (2nd edition revised by H.E. Nørregård-Nielsen), Copenhagen 1976

ROHDE 1993
H.P. Rohde, *Kun en maler. Christen Købke. Breve og optegnelser*, Copenhagen 1993

SCAVENIUS 1994
Bente Scavenius (ed.), *The Golden Age in Denmark: Art and Culture 1800 – 1850*, Copenhagen 1994

SCAVENIUS 1996
Bente Scavenius (ed.), *The Golden Age Revisited: Art and Culture in Denmark 1800–1850*, Copenhagen 1996

SCHWARTZ 1992
Sanford Schwartz, *Christen Købke*, New York 1992

SWANE 1948
Leo Swane, *Christen Købke*, Copenhagen 1948

THORVALDSENS MUSEUM BULLETIN 1997
Stig Miss (ed.), *Thorvaldsens Museum Bulletin 1997*, English edition devoted to Golden Age cultural issues

TØNDBORG 2005
Britta Tøndborg, 'Hanging the Danes: Danish Golden Age Art in a Nineteenth-century Museum Context', *SMK Art Journal*, 2005, pp.119–26

TYBJERG 1996
Hans Tybjerg, *Omkring Købkes Frederiksborg Slot ved aftenbelysning*, Copenhagen 1996

WASHINGTON 2003
Philip Conisbee, et al., *Christoffer Wilhelm Eckersberg 1783–1853*, exhibition catalogue, National Gallery of Art, Washington 2003

WIVEL 1993
Mikael Wivel, *Christen Købke*, Hellerup 1993

WIVEL 2001
Matthias Wivel, 'Face to Face. On Eckersberg's and Købke's Discovery of the Modern', *Statens Museum for Kunst Journal*, vol.5, 2001, pp.50–73

Notes and References

1. Serfdom (*stavnsbåndet*) was enforced in the 1730s. The abolition act of 1788 concerned only boys under fourteen, but was a major step towards the universal freedom instituted in 1849.
2. Most famously Poul Martin Møller's 'Rosen blusser alt i Danas have' ('Roses Glow in Denmark's Garden') of 1820.
3. Jespersen 2004, p.22. See pp.22–6 generally on this issue.
4. Klaus P. Mortensen, 'Demons of the Golden Age. Hans Christian Andersen and Søren Kierkegaard', *Thorvaldsens Museum Bulletin*, 1997, p.12.
5. London 1984, pp.42–3. Gosse visited Denmark in 1872 and 1874.
6. Hans Hertel and Bente Scavenius, 'Home and Abroad, High and Low. Contrasts of the Golden Age', in Scavenius 1996, p.20.
7. Copenhagen 1996, p.101, n.54.
8. On the links between art, science and Golden Age culture, see Bencard 2000.
9. Poulsen 1976, p.59, for instance, says 'we prefer to name the period … after its greatest artist'.
10. London 1984, pp.42, 48, 187 respectively.
11. Hans Edvard Nørregård-Nielsen, 'Conceit and the Golden Age. Oehlenschläger's Grand Tour', in Scavenius 1994, pp.28–9. See also Valdemar Vedel, *Studier over Guldalderen i dansk Digtning*, Copenhagen 1890.
12. Schwartz 1992, p.6.
13. Hannover 1893, pp.22ff, quoted in Copenhagen 1996, p.167. Emil Hannover was a librarian at the Danish Museum of Art & Design, Copenhagen, and its director from 1906. He was subsequently the first director of the Hirschsprung Collection.
14. Købke's quoted letters have been translated for this publication by Sine Krogh from the Danish originals in Rohde 1993. Rohde's work is substantially based on thirty letters in transcript from Hannover's papers in the Danish Museum of Art & Design, supplemented by seventeen letters from the Royal Library, the Record Office (Rigsarkivet), the Royal Danish Academy and Thorvaldsens Museum.
15. See Nørregård-Nielsen 2006, p.27. Copenhagen 1996, pp.98–9, details each family member with dates, biographical information and an attempt to clarify the staggering complexity of the Købke genealogy.
16. See London 1984, p.12; Schwartz 1992, pp.8, 35.
17. Hans Edvard Nørregård-Nielsen, '"Just imagine, Mother Dear". Christen Købke's sister in Rome', in Scavenius 1996, p.116.
18. Quoted in Joakim Garff, 'An Unholy Game with the Holy of Holies. Søren Kierkegaard's Attack on the Church', in Scavenius 1994, p.118.
19. On Kunstforeningen and patronage generally see Berman 2007, pp.56–60.
20. See Emma Salling, *Kunstakademiets guldmedalje konkurrencer 1755–1857*, Copenhagen 1975, p.7 on this issue.
21. The comment on the bad behaviour of apprentices is in Hannover 1893, p.3. Student statistics are listed in F. Meldahl and P. Johansen, *Det kongelige Akademi for de skjønne Kunster 1700–1904*, Copenhagen 1904, p.191.
22. Ibid., p.154.
23. Ibid., pp.138–42.
24. Quotations respectively by Bernhard Maaz, 'Citizens of the World – The Idea of Europe', in *Views on Europe – Europe and German Painting in the Nineteenth Century*, exhibition catalogue, Centre for Fine Arts (BOZAR), Brussels, Ostfildern 2007, pp.48–9; and ibid., Birgit Verwiebe, 'The Northern Light – Scandinavia', p.148.
25. Diary entry of 17 May 1828, quoted in Copenhagen 1996, p.32.
26. On the painting and its studies see Marianne Saabye (ed.), *Wilhelm Bendz: A Young Painter of the Danish Golden Age 1804–1832*, exhibition catalogue, Den Hirschsprungske Samling, 1996, pp.74–7.
27. A chronology of these progressive teaching methods can be found in Copenhagen 1994, pp.172–3.
28. Washington 2003, p.21.
29. Rohde 1993, p.28.
30. On Eckersberg generally see Washington 2003. On his progressive approach and technique see pp.13–26; and Wivel 2001.
31. For a reconstruction see Kasper Monrad, *Købke på Blegdammen og ved Sortedamssøen*, Copenhagen 1981, p.27.
32. Copenhagen 1996, p.118.
33. Both quoted in Washington 2003, p.7.
34. London 1984, p.200.
35. Identification and dates of works exhibited at Charlottenborg are based on information in *Fortegnelse over Danske Kunstneres Arbejder paa de ved Det Kgl. Akademi For De Skønne Kunster i Aarene 1807–1882 Afholdte Charlottenborg-Udstillinger*, Copenhagen 1883; and from the 1833 and 1834 catalogues of *Fortegnelse over de ved det Kongelige Academie for de skjønne Kunster offentligen udstillede Kunstværker*, Copenhagen.
36. Copenhagen 1996, p.34.
37. Information on the casts displayed can be found in Nørregård-Nielsen 1991, p.54.
38. London 1984, p.190.
39. On Købke's life in the Citadel see Copenhagen 1981.
40. I am grateful to Signe Langberg, curator at Vendsyssel Historiske Museum, for this information.
41. Kjørup 1997, p.48, suggests Købke is playing with Alberti's classical idea that a painting represents a window onto the world.

42. Copenhagen 1996, pp.163–4, citing Hannover 1893, pp.66–70.

43. On the issue of cloud studies see Gertrud Hvidberg-Hansen, et al., *Himlens spejl. Skyer og vejrlig i dansk maleri, 1770–1880*, exhibition catalogue, Fyns Kunstmuseum 2002. The relationship of Danish art to Turner and Constable, including Købke's use of cloud and sky studies, is discussed generally in *Turner and Romantic Nature*, exhibition catalogue, Statens Museum for Kunst, Copenhagen 2004. More widely see John Gage, 'Clouds Over Europe', in *Constable's Clouds*, exhibition catalogue, National Gallery of Scotland, Edinburgh 2000, pp.125–34.

44. Copenhagen 1996, p.130.

45. Købke received 100 species (or 200 rigs-daler), a handsome sum when placed in context with other commissions of the same time: 20 species for a portrait and 50 species for another commission, see Rohde 1993, p.35.

46. Ibid., p.34. Here and elsewhere the original character and lack of sophistication of Købke's letters has been retained at the cost of some grammatical correctness. He seems to have regarded punctuation as optional in his not always coherent stream of consciousness. Whilst this can appear inelegant, the tendency to tidy up his writing and give it a more literary and lucid tone distorts the authenticity of his voice.

47. Copenhagen 1996, p.172.

48. Letter to Jørgen Roed, 14 July 1836, in Rohde 1993, p.49.

49. See Wivel 2001, p.68.

50. Nørregård-Nielsen 1995, p.188.

51. *Niels Laurits Høyens Skrifter*, vol. III (ed. J.L. Ussing), Copenhagen 1876.

52. On Høyen and his influence see Berman 2007, pp.96–104; Tøndborg 2005; Jørgen Jensen, 'The Mirror of History. From History Painting to Landscapes', in Scavenius 1994, pp.32–5.

53. Also influential here were the 1802 lectures on natural philosophy by the Norwegian-born Henrik Steffens (1773–1845) published in 1803 as *Indledning til philoso-phiske Forelæsninger*, which popularised similar ideas from Schelling's *Naturphilosophie*, which emerged from 1797.

54. Hans Vammen, '"Schouw is wonderful …" A Professor and his Golden Age Network', in Bencard 2000, p.252.

55. Ibid., pp.254–6.

56. See Kasper Monrad, 'A View Through Three Arches: Danish and German Artists in Denmark, Germany and Italy', in Ottawa, Hamburg, and Copenhagen 1999–2000, pp.8–9.

57. London 1984, p.210.

58. See Hans Hertel, 'Our very own Scotland. The Discovery of Jutland by Danish Literature and Art', in Scavenius 1994, pp.174–85.

59. On the dating and setting of this work see Nørregård-Nielsen 2006, pp.411–13.

60. Tybjerg 1996, p.8.

61. Rohde 1993, p.30.

62. New York, Pittsburgh, and Sacramento 1995–6, p.172.

63. See Tybjerg 1996, pp.86–7, notes 43 and 44 on Dahl's and other versions.

64. Rohde 1993, p.43. Købke means 'Jægerbakken' which is the small hill opposite the lake and castle from where Frederiksborg is viewed in his painting.

65. Ibid., p.37, undated letter of 1835.

66. Ibid., p.35, undated letter of 1834–5.

67. Ibid., pp.43–8, see letters of 12 August, 15 September and 26 October 1835.

68. Ibid., pp.45, 46 respectively.

69. Ibid., p.46, letter of 15 September 1835.

70. Ibid.

71. London 1984, p.212.

72. *Kjøbenhavnsposten (The Copenhagen Post)*. Redigeret og udgivet af A.P. Liunge. 10de Aarg. Tirsdag d. 12 April 1836. No. 107. Translation Sine Krogh. Sibbern presumably refers to the then highly popular Swiss painter and poet of pastoral idylls Salomon Gessner (1730–1788).

73. Ibid.

74. Letters of 11, 14, 15 October, Rohde 1993, pp.51–2.

75. Copenhagen 1996, pp.198–9.

76. Letter of 14 July 1836, Rohde 1993, p.50. Købke does here confess to reading avidly the *Book of Winter Sermons* by Claus Harms (1778–1855), a Lutheran preacher who objected to the prevailing rationalism in religion and whose work was at the time very popular.

77. Tøndborg 2005, p.124.

78. Viben Bech, 'Chemise, Mahogany and Horsehair. Fashions in Furnishing and Dress', in Scavenius 1994, pp.148–55.

79. Nørregård-Nielsen 2006, pp.424, 427.

80. Copenhagen 1996, p.59.

81. London 1984, p.198.

82. Ibid., p.48 for information on the painting's genesis.

83. Copenhagen 1996, p.149.

84. The 1848 auction catalogue of Købke's works includes eighty-four etchings by foreign artists, five by Potter (items 46–50) of cows grazing, standing, even 'A Cow Pissing'! Købke 1848, p.21.

85. Berman 2007, p.63 cites four such works between 1826 and 1830 and another by Blunck.

86. This painting is much discussed in works on Købke and Danish art. See specifically, Jens Peter Munk, *Købke, Sødring og atelieret på Toldbodvejen*, Den Hirschsprungske Samling, Copenhagen 1985; Jürgen Hoppmann, 'Esplanaden 4 – et minderigt hus i København. Ej blot som atelier', pp.103–22 in *Historiske Meddelelser om København*, Copenhagen 1997.

87. Letter of 14 July 1836, in Rohde 1993, p.49.

88. *Kjøbenhavnsposten (The Copenhagen Post)*, Tuesday 12 April 1836.

89. See Kasper Monrad, 'History and Danish Golden Age Painting', in *Thorvaldsens Museum Bulletin 1997*, p.30; Hans Hertel, 'Our very own Scotland. The Discovery of Jutland by Danish Literature and Art', in Scavenius, 1994 p.174.

90. Nørregård-Nielsen 1995, p.202.

91. Rohde 1993, pp.49, 55 respectively.

92. Ibid., pp.86–7; quotation p.95.

93. I am immensely grateful to Kasper Salto for arranging rare access to view the apartment. For more on this unique interior see Ejner Johansson, 'Artistic Circles. Interiors by Frederiksholms Kanal', in Scavenius 1994, pp.82–7.

94. More judicious assessment can be found by Kasper Monrad in Los Angeles, New York, and Copenhagen 1993–4, pp.168–9; and Wivel 1993, pp.26–9.

95. Rohde 1993, p.38.

96. This and further census information taken from Copenhagen 1996, pp.201–3.

97. See Rohde 1993, pp.34–5, 47–8 respectively.

98. Letter of 3 August 1836, quoted in Copenhagen 1996, p.71.

99. See Schwartz 1992, pp.39–42 on Blegdammen and the dining room pictures.

100. Letter of 14 October 1836, Rohde 1993, p.51.

101. Ibid., p.48, letter of 14 July 1836.

102. On the rural-urban aspects of Golden Age life see Margit Mogensen, 'Twixt Town and Country. Markets, Milk and Aquavit', in Scavenius 1994, pp.38–49.

103. Nørregård-Nielsen 2006, p.447, and figs. 80, 81.

104. Rohde 1993, p.51.

105. *Dansk Kunstblad (Danish Art Magazine)* vol. 1, 11 February 1837, No. 24, p.178. Translation Sine Krogh.

106. Jens Peter Jacobsen, *Niels Lyhne* (translation Tiina Nunnally), London 1990, p.33.

107. The philosophical and religious aspects of the work are developed in Wivel 2001.

108. See David Burmeister Kaaring, 'Reality as Icon – The Cottage Motif in Dutch Landscape Painting 1600–1650', in *SMK Art Journal*, 2007, pp.96–107.

109. Copenhagen 1996, pp.243–5.

110. These aspects are picked up in Ottawa, Hamburg, and Copenhagen 1999–2000, p.x, and in Wivel 1993, p.32.

111. *Portefeuillen* 5 May 1839, unpaginated. Translation Sine Krogh.

112. The flag controversy is addressed inconclusively in London 1984, p.218; Geraldine Norman, *Biedermeier Painting*, London 1987, p.97; Berman 2007, p.258, n.59. The flag appears in a modern setting in Eckersberg's view of Kronborg Castle (1829, Statens Museum for Kunst) but is here descriptive of an official state building.

113. See Hans Christian Bjerg, *Dannebrog. Historien om et kristent og nationalt symbol*, Højbjerg 2006, pp.55–6.

114. Klaus P. Mortensen, 'Demons of the Golden Age. Hans Christian Andersen and Søren Kierkegaard', in *Thorvaldsens Museum Bulletin*, 1997, p.96.

115. Dan Ch. Christensen, 'H.C. Ørsted in Paris and Copenhagen', in Scavenius 1994, p.56 summarising Oehlenschläger.

116. Rohde 1993, pp.55, 56.

117. For instance Jørgen I. Jensen, 'An Inner Trembling. The Balance between the Classical World and Romantic Grandeur', in Scavenius 1994, pp.77–8.

118. See Ottawa, Hamburg, and Copenhagen 1999–2000, p.5.

119. Copenhagen 1996, p.283 quotes two separate readings that take the same view.

120. See two letters of 5 October 1837 seeking funds from the foundation and a reference from Købke's tutors to apply for a scholarship, as well as the recommendation letter of 16 October 1837 signed by, amongst others, Eckersberg, C.F. Hansen, J.L. Lund, Freund and Høyen, Rohde 1993, pp.52–3. On the foundation see Henny Glarbo, *Fonden Ad Usus Publicos. Aktmæssige Bidrag til Belysning af dens Virksomhed, Bind 3. Udgivet af Rigsarkivet*, Ejnar Munksgaards Forlag, Copenhagen 1947, pp.519–20, 657.

121. Nørregård-Nielsen, '"Just imagine, Mother Dear". Christen Købke's sister in Rome', p.116. This highly entertaining article (pp.110–17) gives many amusing insights into artists travelling to Rome.

122. Letter of 27 October 1834, Rohde 1993, pp.34–5.

123. See Maaz note 24, p.149.

124. Letter of 28 December 1837, Rohde 1993, p.54.

125. Ibid., p.66, letter of 16 February 1839.

126. Copenhagen 1996, p.305.

127. Ibid., p.327.

128. Letter of 17 October 1841, Rohde 1993, p.98.

129. Copenhagen 1996, pp.327–9.

130. Letter of 25 October 1841, Rohde 1993, p.101.

131. Købke worked on ceilings in Roman rooms II, V, VI and XLI. See Nørregård-Nielsen 2006, pp.734–42. On the Puggaard decorations see p.797.

132. Letter of 25 April 1846, Rohde 1993, p.115. On the portrait more generally see Nørregård-Nielsen 2006, pp.789–90.

133. On Eckersberg and meteorological studies within a European context see Washington 2003, pp.45–6, 136–9.

134. Wivel 1993, p.44.

135. Hannover 1893, pp.120–2.

136. Nørregård-Nielsen 2006, p.798. Translation Sine Krogh.

137. Ibid., pp.797–803, for information on Købke's death, funeral and the auction of his works. For the auction catalogue see Købke 1848.

138. On these aspects see Wivel 1993, pp.45–7.

139. Sune Auken, 'Nature as a Sign. Grundtvig and science', in Bencard 2000, pp.217, 220.

140. Linnet 2003, p.423.

141. Linnet 2001, p.64.

142. Plato, *The Republic*, Book VI, 501.

143. Rohde 1993, p.34.

144. Quoted in London 1984, p.216.

145. Both quotes in Copenhagen 1996, p.167.

146. Rohde 1993, p.36.

147. Ibid., p.105, letter of 24 June 1845.

IN ITALY · PAGES 104–13

1. Hannover 1893, p.94.
2. Ibid., p.106.
3. Nørregård-Nielsen 1996, vol.3: *Italien tur-retur*, pp.10–131. An abbreviated version is in Copenhagen 1996, pp.77–87.
4. See Nørregård-Nielsen in Copenhagen 1996, pp.78–9.
5. Quoted in Los Angeles, New York, and Copenhagen 1993–4, p.66.
6. See Rohde 1993, p.66; the quote is from the English translation in Copenhagen 1996, p.78.
7. See Copenhagen 1996, cats 142a–142k.
8. On Eckersberg as an open-air painter see Washington 2003, pp.13–25.
9. Copenhagen 1996, cats 134a and 134b.
10. See Raffaello Causa, *Il paesaggio napoletano nella pittura straniera*, exhibition catalogue, Palazzo Reale, Naples 1962 and Anna Ottina Cavina et al., *Paysages d'Italie.*

Les peintres du plein air 1780–1830/Un paese incantato. Italia dipinta da Thomas Jones a Corot, exhibition catalogue, Grand Palais, Paris and Palazzo Te, Mantua 2001.

11. Anne-Birgitte Fonsmark, 'Købke på Capri', *Meddelelser fra Ny Carlsberg Glyptotek*, vol.39, 1983, pp.78–81 (summary in English) and Copenhagen 1996, p.301.

12. This was first suggested in Monrad 2002, pp.15–16; and further developed in Kasper Monrad, *Turner and Romantic Nature*, exhibition catalogue, Statens Museum for Kunst, Copenhagen 2004, pp.139 and 189, note 84.

13. Sigurd Willoch, 'Thomas Fearnley og de danske malere i Italia', *Kunst og Kultur*, vol.64, 1981, pp.249–57.

14. See Torsten Gunnarsson, *Friluftsmåleri före friluftsmåleriet. Oljestudien i nordiskt landskapsmåleri 1800–1850* (Acta Universitatis Upsaliensis. Ars Suetica 12, with an English summary, 'Open-Air Sketching in Scandinavia 1800–1850'), Uppsala 1989, p.230.

15. Monrad 2006, pp.115–17.

16. See Alistair Smith et al., '*Nature's Way*'. *Romantic Landscapes from Norway*, exhibition catalogue, The Whitworth Art Gallery, Manchester and The Fitzwilliam Museum, Cambridge 1993, cat.28.

17. See Ottawa, Hamburg, and Copenhagen 1999–2000, cat.35 and Købke's *View of Cliffs from Marina Piccola on Capri* (Museum of Fine Arts, Boston; see note 4).

18. Monrad 2002, pp.15–16, and figs 6 and 7.

19. Los Angeles, New York, and Copenhagen 1993–4, cat.75.

20. See New York, Pittsburgh, and Sacramento 1995–6, cat.43.

21. Ibid., cat.44. See also Copenhagen 1996, cat.156. Fearnley painted a study of the Forum in Pompeii from almost the same position, see Sigurd Willoch, *Thomas Fearnley 1802–1842*, exhibition catalogue, The Modum Trust's Blaafarveværk, Modum 1986, cat.68.

22. See Krohn 1915.

23. I did not fully realise the importance of the Italian travels until the paintings were displayed at the 1996 exhibition at the Statens Museum for Kunst. See Monrad 2002, p.17.

Credits ⁓

Index

Page numbers in *italic* denote illustrations. For the purposes of this index Danish letters Ø and Å are filed as if they were English O and A.